BUT FOR THESE MEN

How Eleven Commandos Saved Western Civilisation

John D. Drummond

BUT FOR THESE MEN

THE ELMFIELD PRESS

JOHN D. DRUMMOND

BUT FOR THESE MEN

Originally published in Great Britain
by W. H. Allen 1962

© 1962 John D. Drummond

This edition 1974
ISBN 0 7057 0045 3

A Morley Book published by
The Elmfield Press, Elmfield Road,
Morley, Yorkshire. LS27 ONN

Printed in England
by Stephen Austin and Sons Ltd., Hertford

For
Colonel J. S. Wilson, C.M.G., O.B.E.,
and his gallant group of saboteurs
of the Norwegian section of Special
Operations Executive

CONTENTS

7

ILLUSTRATIONS

Photographs facing pages 64, 96, 113 and 144
by courtesy of Hero Films

CHAPTER 1

Return Ticket to Trouble—By Parachute

"YON'S no yin of oors, Wullie."

"Trawler is."

"The ither isn't. The een is nae sae braw these days. Jimmy! Hey Jimmy! "

The small, intent boy, dangling his mussel-baited hook down into the shoal of saithe on the full of the flood, over the quayside at Aberdeen, that morning of March 17th, 1942, reluctantly surrendered the thin brown twine to a couple of turns around the nearest bollard and dragged his heels across the cobbles.

"Aye, uncle? "

"What's yon flag, laddie? The coaster ahint the trawler." The freckled nose wrinkled in mock disgust.

"Uncle," he wailed. "They were just beginning to bite and ye canna see the Norwegian flag full afore yer eyes."

The two old men, idling, elbow-leaning, along the harbour wall, chewing and spitting, and the boy, three generations apart, did not realise that they were watching the birth of the greatest sabotage campaign of the last war; the beginning of unorthodox military operations by a harried, starved, outnumbered Norwegian group, who saved Britain from atomic bombing by the Nazis. Almost two and a half years before Hiroshima and Nagasaki. . . .

The trawler nudged into her normal berth, after the clackety-clack welcome of the twenty-two inch signalling lamp, over-seeing the port. Barriers were run out by police and security officers to curtain off the disembarkation of the men

11

from the coaster the smaller ship had guided through the inshore minefields on the last few miles of the long, desperate voyage to Scotland.

That foggy March morning of 1942, the 570-ton beat-up old *Galtesund* was the most important ship afloat, in any ocean, and it owed this distinction to one man alone—one out of the twenty-seven Norwegians walking down the gangplank to alien cobbles. Some with mixed feelings.

He was Einar Skinnarland. Professionally, a clever engineer, specialising in dam building, and since the Nazi invasion of his homeland, a burning patriot, hunting around for some way to hit back.

Skinnarland had helped to capture the coaster at gun-point off Flekkefjord. Pistols in the ribs of those they had to overcome had turned the ship away from the normal fjords between Kristiansand and Bergen towards the Scottish fishing-port.

He did not know it when he stepped ashore, but he was the solid answer to the prayers of a group of British Intelligence agents. A native of the Rjukan valley, nestling beneath the forbidding wilderness of the Hardanger Vidda, the aptly named Barren Mountains, four thousand square miles of glaciers, frozen lakes, sudden precipices and nothing much else, he could almost ski as soon as he could toddle.

More important, he was on first-name terms with the top executives of the commandeered Norsk Hydro Electrisk plant, the red question-mark of the world against the Allied war effort.

That was where the heavy water—deuterium oxide—drip-dripped into containers destined for Germany, midwife to the first atomic bomb ever.

Skinnarland was, of course, unaware that the Ministry of Economic Warfare had for some weeks past been filtering information to the British Cabinet based on intelligence reports from Stockholm and other embassies about which there was grave concern. These reports all pointed to one sinister conclusion.

Within the next few hours the Norwegian was to learn

quite a lot. He found himself being questioned by a mildly-spoken security agent who examined such papers as he carried and then returned them to him with a smile.

"We know all about you from mutual friends in London," he said as he offered Skinnarland a cigarette.

Later he heard much of what had been planned for him as he rested in the sleeping compartment of a night express that sped southwards.

His strange companion, whom he could just glimpse through a door-way lit by a dim blue light, warned him that the Nazis were believed to be ahead in the race to perfect the first atom bomb.

The agent's voice was barely audible above the thump of the carriage wheels as they raced towards London but Skinnarland heard him say that recently the Nazis, scenting triumph, had ordered an all-out production drive from the seven-storeyed, reinforced concrete factory that he, Skinnarland, had watched so often from the homes of his parents and friends.

The Norwegian could see it at that moment, by closing his eyes to the tourist poster for Scotland on the opposite wall. A plant literally carved from a mountain side, flourishing like some monstrous cactus, a threatening evil growth. Tucked away. Bomb-defying.

Approached only by a swaying, guarded suspension bridge from the east; by the back door from the south, along a rusting railway line up the Rjukan valley.

As the wayside stations flashed past, scarcely visible through the black-out curtains of their carriage, the man across the communicating door talked far into the swift-rushed night.

Skinnarland began to fully appreciate the big international picture.

"When we get in we'll go straight to the Special Operations Executive headquarters—and see if anybody is around that early," said his guide. "Just a short cab ride. Two men want to see you there. I've ordered tea and biscuits. Lock your door. Sleep well. Good night."

The engineer dozed a little, off and on. He never slept

properly. The past week had been too crowded with impossible happenings.

That single fir cone, idly kicked off the cat-walk over the Møsvatn dam, which he helped supervise in the mountainous Telemark region, had set him off on the long road to London. The swiftly-flowing current had whirled the cone away, over and down to Norsk Hydro far below, where Norwegian power was harnessed to the production of the vital heavy water.

Damn the Germans! He was escaping to Britain to fight back.

His mind made up, he passed the word through the local Milorg, the Resistance movement, that he would join a group hiding from the Gestapo in the Flekkefjord area.

The enemy net was slowly closing around Odd Starheim[1] and his four companions. They planned escape across the North Sea somehow.

Skinnarland made contact at the small sea port, to find the hunted men planning to buy or steal a fishing boat.

Three factors changed this scheme. There was great need for a hasty departure. The coast had been buffeted by gales and the bad weather looked like continuing. Thirdly, all seaworthy vessels of any size were very much under the eyes of the enemy garrison, limited to inshore fishing in the daylight hours only.

They talked together far into the night.

"Goebbels says that if you must lie, make it the outsize of lies," said Starheim, to the men around the table. "If we have to risk stealing a ship, we must aim higher than a fishing cobble. What about hi-jacking the *Galtesund* next time she berths here?"

Most of them knew the coaster. Some had sailed in her in days of leisurely peace, in and out of fjords, dropping cattle, sheep and visiting relatives at wooden jetties up and down the rugged indented coastline when the tides were right.

---

[1] Later, Major Starheim, D.S.O. In August, 1940, with two young volunteers for the exiled forces, he steered the aptly named *The Viking* into Aberdeen. He returned to his homeland by rubber dinghy from a Clyde-based submarine.

Rather like the MacBrayne steamers of Scotland, meandering from the Clyde through the Western Isles to the Outer Hebrides.

The Norwegians pooled their impressions and ideas, half-convinced, wanting to be convinced, that the audacious plot could succeed.

Local fishermen, whose support they had, sneaked in through the back door of the meeting house, filled in the blanks.

Their only reward for risking their lives after curfew was a glass of light gravity beer. They asked for nothing more.

Soon the table was littered with empty bottles and foam-encrusted glasses. But the conspirators had a clear outline of the coaster traced in beer stains by different thumbs.

Starheim transferred all this to paper. Then swayed back in his seat.

"There's almost certain to be shooting, but that's a risk we have to take. A vote? In favour?"

There was general agreement and Starheim then began to rehearse everybody in the positions they were to take up when he gave the signal. Additional weapons, secured from underground sources, were handed round and arrangements were made for a contact to secure the necessary passenger tickets.

Six of them waited together in the shadows until the last minute before going aboard and, although they were unaware of it, luck was with them, for not a single German passenger had been picked up at the previous port of call and this considerably lessened the odds against their chances.

Starheim took a quick look round and saw that his little band would have to deal with about twenty men. They looked a tough bunch with faces scarred and battered in waterfront brawls. As unobtrusively as they could, Starheim's men took up their positions. Three of them were to rush the wheel-house and the remainder were so disposed as to prevent the crew from reaching each other. Near the engine-room hatch one man waited with two revolvers tucked into a belt beneath his coat, while at the rails another stood looking shorewards but not really seeing the coast-line that he might never glimpse again.

The *Galtesund* moved slowly away and turned towards the open sea. As soon as she was well clear, the leader's whistle shrilled and Starheim led the raid on the wheel-house. He stuck a gun into the ribs of the helmsman and told him to keep quiet.

The captain, a burly, formidable man who had been bending over a chart, was less amenable to surrendering the ship. He straightened up and, guns or no guns, began furiously to wrestle with Starheim's aides as they closed in on him.

"There was a bit of trouble for a time," Starheim told the interrogating Naval officer ashore later. "He was a fine man, but our fellows had to sit on him to bring him to his senses."

In other parts of the *Galtesund* guns in steady hands stopped short any further signs of nervous reaction to the coup.

Four shocked men, playing cards in the passenger space, looked up and blinked in outraged disbelief, when an incisive voice in their own tongue said from the doorway: —

"Put your hands flat down on the table please," and then added, with the suggestion of a chuckle, "you can put the hands you are holding face down too, if you feel you are winning. It's a long way to the north of Scotland."

There was no interference from the engine-room because there had been no telegraphed signals from the bridge.

The long and bitter argument centred around the wheel-house. Then Starheim[1] gave the order which turned the bows towards Aberdeen.

---

[1] "Odd Starheim lived up to his first name," says Colonel J. S. Wilson, C.M.G., O.B.E., wartime chief of the Norwegian Section of the Special Operations Executive. "He was a remarkable man. A born seaman, a great resistance organiser, a patriot to his fingertips. Yet, during his infrequent leaves in Britain he travelled to Liverpool to help, in humble fashion, the chaplain at a seamen's mission there. His third break-back from Norway, through enemy patrol boat lines and Luftwaffe coastal cover, was indeed unlucky. We heard nothing for a time, except rumours of bombing. Then his body was washed ashore in Sweden. He was identified by his wrist-watch. Our people abroad managed to arrange for his burial in the village where he was born."

Confident, earlier, of the ultimate success of his sea-going smash-and-grab, the resistance leader had left a terse message for the Admiralty with a telegraphist friend ashore. As he remembered it afterwards he explained that he had stolen a Norwegian coaster and was heading for Aberdeen. Please would they do something to help?

Thus he avoided breaking radio silence, which might have brought Luftwaffe retribution above his mast-head.

The message was received on the night of March 15th in the underground room of the Admiralty, whose questing radio masts overhead picked up eagerly, like the hungry pigeons in nearby Trafalgar Square, any crumb of comfort in those dark times.

The duty officer in Operations Room immediately grabbed the scrambler telephone and called for air cover.

He did not appreciate how important the prize would become to the Allied war effort but he cursed nevertheless when the report came back that all suitable airfields were fogged over and take-offs delayed.

Around this time a monitoring station in Surrey passed along a routine, low priority message that Oslo radio station had broadcast in German, then Norwegian, that a coaster named the *Galtesund* was overdue at her next port of call, but that she was believed to have sought the protection of some fjord or island from a mounting gale.

The jig-saw began to piece together.

"That gives her a breathing space maybe," said the senior naval officer in Operations to his opposite number in R.A.F. uniform.

"We'll get cover off at first chance," was the reply.

But it was not until the afternoon of March 16th that a lucky sighting by a Hudson of Coastal Command pin-pointed the small ship labouring through the white crests far below.

The pilot of the stubby little aircraft had had a briefing which puzzled him a little. All this fuss over that!

He did not know that secret radio sets had been busy again, that there had been many exchanges between Naval Intelligence and the Special Operations Executive, as the growing

B

importance of the breakaway from Flekkefjord came into sharper focus.

"Escort target ship when found to—" he rechecked the ringed North Sea position. "Guide trawler will rendezvous."

The *Galtesund* had no guns—but a signal lamp of sorts.

To his "Welcome" triggered from the Aldis, came back—"Greetings. Many thanks."

Starheim, who held a master's ticket, had taken over the navigation long before. The instructions he was now receiving were acknowledged as the little bullet in the sky whistled lower to give the ship closer protection.

The pilot was well aware of two main dangers to a successful landfall by his charge. A lurking U-boat pressing home a gloaming attack or the chance discovery by a long-range enemy fighter-bomber.

To the Norwegian below there was a third factor, perhaps more worrying. He had no charts for the area. There were thick minefields ahead.

The sight of the Hudson, swooping ahead was small comfort.

The last time Starheim had sailed into Aberdeen he had been at the tiller of a small, shallow-draft boat. Now he was taking in a ship drawing a great deal of water and completely unprotected against mines, magnetic or otherwise.

The next flashed signal from the patrol aircraft did nothing to cheer him up.

"Forced return to base. Fuel problem."

He wearily acknowledged the message. He had not slept for more than a few minutes in forty-eight hours.

The lamp above blinked again.

"Here's your night nurse."

A relief Hudson was approaching astern.

At first light the trawler found them, with the faithful guardian still overhead.

The fog which had defeated an earlier convoy by Coastal Command might have been a blessing in disguise after all, Starheim reckoned. Protection too near the coast he had left might well have alerted the enemy.

Like so many Norwegians he knew quite a few Scottish catchphrases.

"Lead on, MacDuff," he murmured below his breath. Gratefully, he called out the course correction necessary to follow the smaller ship.

A seaman in the trawler looked up from swabbing the deck.

"Norwegians," he said laconically to his nearest shipmate. "Handy drinkers. Means less of that rationed beer for us. Aye well."

It was in this way that Skinnarland had reached Aberdeen in the *Galtesund*.[1]

Skinnarland, a methodically-minded man, punched his railway pillow into more comfortable shape and listened to the contented snoring from the other compartment. The agent's job was nearly over. His was just beginning.

As early as the autumn of 1939 there had been talk relayed from Berlin that German scientists were openly discussing the importance of heavy water production in any future war.

Rumours had run through his native valley that agents of the French Secret Service—the Deuxième Bureau—had bought and smuggled from Norway small pre-invasion stocks. One of the Norsk Hydro directors involved in the deal had told his family: —"If the Germans ever invade our country you must get away. I shall be among the first to be shot."

As things turned out, the containers were shipped from France to London a few hours before Panzers were rolling along French roads. By then physicists in Germany, Britain, America, and France too, were already seeking the elusive clue to the harnessing of nuclear chain-reaction.

Skinnarland recalled the engineers below his dam—many of them boyhood friends—who had been ordered in May,

---

[1] The *Galtesund* was an old but sturdy coaster. Until the end of the shooting in Europe, she steamed around alien coasts, on the orders of the Norwegian Shipping Authority, regardless of danger. She was owned by the Arendal Steamship Company of Arendal, Norway, when captured. After a lay-up in Loch Ryan, off Stranraer, Scotland, she was returned to her owners and traded between Oslo and Bergen until 1956 and was then sold to overseas buyers.

1940, to step up production of the deuterium oxide to 3,000 lb a year, or else!

He guessed, as the train stopped in a tunnel for the air-raid "enemy overhead" warning, at the identity of one of the men waiting to greet him: Professor Leif Tronstad,[1] who had played a major part in designing the Norsk Hydro plant.

The second man he had heard well about, but never met, was Colonel J. S. Wilson, head of the Norwegian Section of the Special Operations Executive. He believed that Wilson had been extending undercover operations against the Nazis in Norway since the beginning of the year.

The engineer was right on both counts. After the call from behind the locked door, the tea and one biscuit and the swaying shave he queued with his guide for a taxi. They were dropped at Chiltern Court, the requisitioned block of London flats which served as S.O.E. headquarters.

Despite the early hour—the express from the north had caught up on the raids and arrived only a few minutes late—they were expected.

The guide drifted away with a nod of farewell as Skinnarland was warmly received by Professor Tronstad and then introduced to his colleague, who turned out to be Colonel Wilson. He was a small but tough-looking man with a pleasant smile and he apologised for not knowing Norwegian when Tronstad turned from his native language and began to speak in English. The professor said to Skinnarland:

"There are two questions we want to ask you. To begin with do you think that you will be missed by now?"

"I don't think so. I had let it be known that I was going into the hills on a hunting trip."

Tronstad nodded approvingly and Wilson then took over and put the other question:

"Are you prepared, with what training we can give you in the time available, to parachute back to the Hardanger Vidda

---

[1] Later. Major Tronstad, O.B.E., of the Norwegian High Command. He was ambushed and killed by a Norwegian traitor at the beginning of the Liberation. He had returned to his homeland to prevent the destruction of important installations such as the Vemork factory by the Nazis.

before you are missed? We want to be kept posted about progress at Vemork."

Without hesitation Skinnarland nodded.

"I'm afraid," cautioned the Intelligence chief, "that you are tackling a very tough assignment. There is not an hour to lose. And I can't promise you any immediate help. Others— some of whom you know—will follow later. But, quite frankly, we are greatly worried about what's going on at Norsk Hydro. The Nazis have just demanded 10,000 lb of heavy water by Christmas. And you'll appreciate what kind of present that might lead to, over London."

Tronstad gave a wry smile as he spoke again.

"You will, I hope, be contributing to the utter destruction of a dream I helped to create. But it is necessary. Just take a look at this."

He led Skinnarland across to a blown-up photograph of the plant the engineer knew so well from a distance.

"There." The finger stabbed into the bowels of the seven storeyed building. "That is where all the trouble in the western world could come from, very soon."

"Don't jump into this with your eyes shut," warned Wilson. "Parachuting is a tricky business. And we won't have much time to give you the chance to become an expert."

It was just eleven days after reaching Aberdeen that Einar Skinnarland, now a properly commissioned subaltern, headed homewards again in a Halifax bomber. To hand was a suitcase radio, for he had achieved a slow but accurate sending rate in radio telegraphy.

Throughout the flight he sat with the weapons that had been issued to him cradled in his arms. He had been an excellent marksman from boyhood. Occasionally he would glance at his parachute, dreading a moment to come. He had experienced just one push-in-the-back jump from the training balloon at Ringway Airport, Manchester.

CHAPTER 2

Descent By Moonlight

S KINNARLAND felt the loneliest man in the world that
moon-lit morning of March 29th, 1942.

Around him the bomber crew went about their familiar jobs—seven men whose task it was to arrive over a pencil point in Norway, a place unknown to them before, and see to it that their solitary passenger was dropped at the precise moment.

The Norwegian, hardly aware how intently he was listening to the muffled rhythm of the plane's engines, began to rehearse again, like an anxious actor in the wings. Only a few minutes before the pilot had signalled to him and dipped a gloved thumb downwards to indicate they were crossing the coast-line—less than one hour's flying time.

Skinnarland said to himself: " Feet together and launch off gently. Relax every muscle when you hit the silk and when you land. Tuck up your legs and go down on your knees. Watch for the wind-snatch. Get rid of the 'chute as quickly as you can."

He was about to make wartime history in his drop by bright moonlight—the first man to parachute into that part of Norway since the German invasion.

He knew intimately the terrain of what he dubbed " my Rjukan back-yard " and was aware of the dangers. A few yards in the wrong direction and he would plunge, maybe suffocated by his own means of delivery, into a half-frozen lake, or bowl over a precipice, bringing down an avalanche of boulders and snow atop of him.

Norway was the parachutist's nightmare for the Special Operations Executive headquarters in London. Skinnarland had jumped just once before, from the tame, captive balloon at Manchester. And below, he knew, there were enemy patrols criss-crossing the country on skis, alert to anything that might drop from the clouds.

"Five minutes to the drop area," the pilot had warned him over the intercom.

"I'll count down when I have pin-pointed the spot." Then he had added, in a carefully acquired Norwegian phrase "Skål far Vikingene".

"I needed all the luck that was going and knew it," the first of the British-launched saboteurs told his friends later. "It wasn't that easy trying to keep up courage."

He dangled his legs out of the launching hole at the shoulder-tap signal.

"It is just like a lavatory seat," grinned the man who was helping him. "Only I'm the one who pulls the plug."

It was a corny wisecrack but it took the edge off the tension.

Skinnarland was welcomed by the yielding whiteness of his own countryside. "It was quite peaceful floating down, after the noise of the bomber had died away," he recalls. "I was lucky in landing."

He dropped within easy walking distance of his isolated home and later found that his absence had gone unnoticed.

Only six men knew the reason for his rapid return, the quick turnround from the Galtesund's berthing at Aberdeen.

He resumed, smoothly enough, his old job as engineer, putting in each day the hours he was forced to work. So far as he was able to judge there was not a shadow of suspicion against him, but he was extremely cautious and, in playing a waiting game, relied on what he saw and heard. His studied care did not however prevent him from making further contacts with the top executives of Norsk Hydro and he was able to transmit the information he gathered to Chiltern Court through the Milorg organisation in the Oslo area.

Skinnarland gradually improved his channels of communications by way of the Swedish border and the diplomatic bags from Stockholm.

He sent accurate but alarming information as the weeks went past. With everything but guns at the napes of their necks the men in the Rjukan valley were being pressured into increasing that drip-drip of heavy water to the holding containers.

The engineer knew there could be no reinforcements from Britain, because of the short hours of darkness, for a matter of months.

Again, as when he slid from the Halifax, he felt very, very lonely. A man guarding one of the biggest secrets of the war.

He was big was Skinnarland, even measured against those native mountains he knew so intimately. Broad across the shoulders, like the dams he helped build, and cool-headed, as the snow caps up above.

Yet, for three tensed-up years, Germans were breathing down his neck every other day of the week, without thawing away any of his great courage.

He had been given a second job in life. A war-time job he wanted.

Skinnarland guesses—dates and names have rightly, perhaps, vanished from the secret files, as Allied agents swallowed the death pill or just floated face down in some canal or river, with a bullet in their brains—that he was probably the longest established man on the right spot in occupied Europe for the British War Cabinet. He makes no boast of this. His fellow saboteurs sketch in the details.

The secret gear from Britain was hidden in a family summer hut some miles from the dam he tended. Firing squad for how many?—if found by a roving enemy patrol—he wondered, every time he turned the key in the door after a visit.

From the Møsvass watershed he risked the dip down into the Rjukan valley regularly; to talk and joke over the rationed drinks with the men who knew exactly what was happening inside Norsk Hydro and to hear the latest information about German movements from youngsters like Leif Per Longum.[1]

The surrounding countryside was perhaps in their favour. At least in the beginning. Thousands of years ago there was a split in the earth's crust about two hundred miles north-east from what is now Oslo.

"Two hundred miles as the crow flies," grumbled Einar Skinnarland to his brother over his communication difficulties. "But at least birds don't need snow ploughs half the time."

Down the years, down the gorge, the river Maan has poured into the fjord and the sea, without eroding the sheer, precipitous faces on either side by more than a few inches.[2]

The suspension bridge is the only crossing between Vemork and Rjukan, four miles downhill, where the valley flattens out. Beyond the bridge, to the north, the steep foothills, with pine and fir trees needling the sky, ascend to the heights of the Hardanger Vidda, reindeer country. Skinnarland knew few Germans had penetrated into this wilderness. For the local garrison civilisation ended with the Norsk Hydro.

By courier to Oslo, by a second resistance runner to Malmö —who had the information on ricepaper plastered to his spine —by yet another to Stockholm, the engineer-agent drew a word picture of the target area. Contact after contact within the plant contributed.

Skinnarland, methodically-minded, was staggered by the deductions he was forced to draw from their details. He checked and double-checked a blueprint of sudden death.

Only fifteen enemy guards, semi-illiterate, third-rate troops,

---

[1] Leif Longum, at the age of twenty-seven, became second-in-command of Milorg for the whole area during the uprising.

[2] In places a kicked stone drops down six hundred feet, without obstruction until it hits the water or ice below.

General Sir Andrew Thorne, one-time General-officer-Commanding, Scotland, later Commander-in-Chief, Norway, craned his neck upwards and told Colonel Wilson beside him: —

"I thought you had been spinning me a fairy story. Had I seen this place I would have considered the venture outright madness."

The Nazis thought the gorge impassable. Workers in the ravine factories, where the sun never shines during the winter months, think it fairly impossible.

non-Norwegian speaking, skimpy overcoats muffling their ears, and hearing, had been recruited to protect one of the most vital objectives in this or any other war.

"They depend too much on the surrounding natural defences," he reported to London. "The Germans are in the hut-barracks between the main machinery room and the electrolysis plant. Change of guard is 1800-2000 hours, around the likely time of attack. Normally two Germans on the bridge. During an alarm, three patrols inside the factory area and flood-lighting on the road between Vemork and Vaaer." (Nearest inhabited area, but just a collection of hill-clinging timbered houses.)

"Normally, there are only two Norwegian guards inside the factory area at night, plus one at the main gates and one roving. All doors into the electrolysis factory locked, except one which opens into the yard.

"The night guard is usually Georg Nyhus, a middle-aged, decent fellow. A neighbour. He should not be hurt. His only job is to check the permits of workers through his window, after they have been cleared by the two sentries on the bridge."

Colonel Wilson and Professor Tronstad in London became two anxious men as the eyes and ears of Britain in the vital valley, through messages and sketches, gradually brought into sharp focus the position at Norsk Hydro. And Wilson did not worry easily.

In 1921, when the late Lord Baden-Powell visited India, he thought he recognised in the smiling, unruffled District Scout Commissioner in Calcutta a future world leader of the movement. His man was also Senior Deputy Police Commissioner in the city and deeply involved in counter-espionage at the time.

The chance came sooner than either of the men concerned expected.

There were sweeping, some local critics said, stupid, changes in the set-up of the Indian Police forces. Wilson resigned on December 31st, 1922, and returned to England to take over the international scouting camp at Gilwell Park in the Epping Forest for fifteen years.

With a second Munich unlikely, he offered his services in 1939 for the war just over the horizon, plus those of many senior Scouts or Rovers, trained in all means of signalling. The Admiralty accepted the promise of these recruits with alacrity, within twenty-four hours of the telephone call. Wilson himself, though, was sent with others by the Army on an undercover mission to Jugoslavia and did not return until many weeks later.

How did he drift into the cloak-and-dagger, twilight world of the Service known as Special Operations Executive?

At the age of seventy-three Colonel Wilson still maintains the traditional silence, with impish grin. Friends, like Major-General Sir Colin Gubbins, K.C.M.G., D.S.O., M.C., help with the answer.

Wilson, police trained in the war against smugglers, crooks and enemy agents in the Far East, had also experienced the rigours of some of the wildest country in the world and knew, therefore, what was required of both himself and those he would send on secret missions.

Special Operations Executive was born in August, 1940, on a directive from the War Cabinet. The founders, drawn from the network of the interlinked existing Intelligence services, reinforced by men—and women—with the oddest qualifications, were charged with the job of undermining the enemy effort, by subversive action in territories already occupied or likely to be taken over. To destroy, by any means possible, men, material and morale.

Colonel Wilson was given the task, in October of that year, of drawing up the training blueprint for the relentless battle of the future. He began without a single recruit for the ventures that lay ahead, but what he laid down remained unchanged until the end of the European war, even to the first atomic bomb over Hiroshima.

When he was transferred, to take charge of the Norwegian section of S.O.E., in January, 1942, he inherited a legacy of Viking bravery. What successes had been achieved had been won desperately but there had been, too, grim failures against a mass of enemy troops whose lines stretched the length and width of a country nearly twice the stretch of Scotland and

England together, a narrow-waisted land, with the distance between the North Cape and Lindesnes in the south almost as far as that from the latter town to the Pyrenees.

Exactly a week before the Nazi invasion of Norway four undercover agents infiltrated from Britain into that strange, romantic country of fjords, glaciers and snow-capped mountains, brief summer nights and long dark winter days. They were the forerunners of the Special Operations Executive, but had, in fact, received their orders from M.I. (R) branch, to which they were attached. They can now be identified as —Captain J. Watt Torrance, who went to Narvik; Major Palmer (Trondheim, afterwards the hiding place of the pocket battleship *Tirpitz*); Captain Andrew Croft (Bergen); and Captain Malcolm Munthe, a relative of the author-philosopher, and an agent who was later to play a major role in the Stockholm-Scotland clearing centre. He went to Stavanger at that time.

The four had orders to establish secret radio link-ups with London and to prepare for the reception of small, highly-trained military groups the moment they received the "Beltor" wireless signal.

Panzer units beat them to the punch by a matter of hours. Torrance helped in the evacuation of the British Consulate, and then joined the Allied forces when they finally reached Narvik. He remained there, fighting in the mountains, until the last withdrawal.

Major Palmer was captured, but Captain Croft was absorbed into the first unit to reach his area, and pulled out with them when the odds were hopelessly against them.

Munthe helped to burn the secret files of the Consulate at his port and organised a fishing boat to take the staff across the North Sea. Although wounded in the leg, he contacted the Norwegian forces in the South and fought with his countrymen in a series of retreating actions between April 22nd and the black day of May 5th.

Of the four agents two only returned to Britain. The information they brought back, some of it based on what they had been told by Norwegian industrialists, showed the shape of things quickly to come. Norway, its three million people, its specialised plant and technicians, was due to be exploited to the full by the Nazis. But however grave and disquieting all this was, and it had to be considered against a background of military defeat in which British and Norwegian forces had suffered grievous losses and the civilian population the terror and tyranny of the Gestapo, Norway was by no means utterly crushed.

Proof of an unquenchable spirit was made manifest by those men who streamed across the North Sea to this country in all kinds of small craft from cobles to small cabin cruisers and, on one almost unbelievable occasion, in a canoe and just a couple of paddles. These men were the true upholders of freedom whom defeat could not discourage.

Valour, too, was to be found among thousands of men and women who had, perforce, to remain behind. They were always prepared to do much more than wait for the day of liberation. Ostensibly, they had submitted to the invaders but they were eager to help—if they could. They needed direction and inspiration from without—from Britain and her Allies.

This was the problem facing Colonel Wilson when Norway became the objective of the Special Operations Executive. He himself could speak no more than a few words of Norwegian properly, but he saw what lay between the lines, as he thumbed through reports of small half-organised pockets of defiance and individual heroism across the sea.

His first two officers in the Norwegian Section, Major P. W. T. Broughton-Leigh and Lieutenant J. L. Chaworth-Mushers, R.N.V.R., whose farm had been over-run by the Germans, had been friends from their schooldays. They knew the occupied territory well.

Their first six recruits for training as agents were Odd Starheim, of the *Viking* episode, and his two crew mates Konrad Lindberg and Frithof Pedersen, plus Ruben Larsen (already a veteran of a raid back from the Shetlands to destroy power stations and pipe-lines and pylons on the Norwegian coast), Gunnar Fougner and Nils Nordland.

These were the first half dozen. Scores were to follow. The

man who became a legend, after his death from a sniper's bullet, whose name is immortalised in that of a crack Company of the Royal Norwegian Army, stepped ashore in Britain during September, 1940. Lieutenant Martin Linge[1] had been wounded in his own country but immediately volunteered to Special Operations Executive and began screening and training picked men for the Norwegian Section.

The intake was between twenty and twenty-five each month during 1941.

Linge, until his death, became the driving force in the field behind the group, while Colonel Wilson and his staff, sorely tried at times, fought the paper battles of Whitehall, attempting to justify their unorthodox methods of warfare in critical and often cynical circles.

In early 1941 a holding depot at Fawley Court, near Henley-on-Thames, was reluctantly handed over and other accommodation had to be found.

Three houses were picked out—Drumintoul Lodge, Glenmore Lodge and Forest Lodge, eight miles apart—near faraway Aviemore, Inverness-shire, in the Scottish Highlands. They not only met the needs of the growing force of earnest Norwegians from every walk of life, but were on the fringe of the Cairngorms, where the climate for several months of the year, and snow conditions for weeks at a time, more closely resembled their homeland than any place in the British Isles.

Colonel Wilson explains: "Even the most expert British skiers, and we didn't have many, could not have lived in the mountains across the North Sea. Again, how many trained Allied soldiers could speak fluent Norwegian? It would have been suicide to have parachuted our own people over on

---

[1] Captain Martin Linge, D.S.C., was killed in a Commando-style raid at Maaloy on 27th December, 1941. He was avenged by his sergeant, Ruben Larsen, who shot the sniper and burned down the German headquarters. Captain Linge is buried in Maaloy cemetery.
" He was that madly adventurous and patriotic type who make the best of soldiers—yet before the war he was one of Norway's most popular actors," says Colonel Wilson. " His death was a great blow to our growing organisation. In his honour permission was granted to issue ' Linge ' shoulder flashes to the Company he had helped to train. In 1944 his only son escaped through Sweden to join his father's old unit. He went on active service, was taken prisoner but finally escaped back to England."

sabotage work. The enemy would have known about the landings in a matter of days, if not hours. Don't forget there were a few Quislings over there as well as many loyalists.

"And Norway, geographically, and in every other way, was just about the worst country in the world for undercover operations. The weather could change from favourable to decidedly dangerous in a few minutes. Areas suitable for landings, away from the flat country occupied by the Germans, were few and far between. Railways and roads, in places where we had some interest, were almost non-existent. It was a country for mountain-trained men, who could merge into the local background, minutes after they hit the deck."

From their hush-hush base the young Norwegians gladly accepted the challenge of the alien forests and moors around.

"Live off the land for a week at a time," ordered London.

The stags and elks back home had bigger antlers than the deer which fell to their British Lee-Enfields but they were hearty eaters and the meat tasted much the same. The men varied their diet with salmon poached from the rivers. They were taken with rod and line when time did not matter and blasted to the surface of the pools with handgrenades when they were hungry.

Often pheasant or grouse helped eke out their issue of bare survival rations. The code-name "Grouse"—*Rype* in their own language—became of deepening significance to four of them at Aviemore as the September nights of 1942 drew out in lengthening darkness.

They were Jens Poulsson and Claus Helberg, boyhood chums from the Rjukan valley, Arne Kjelstrup, another local man, who had left for Oslo as a youngster, and Knut Haugland, who knew the district well, both in summer and winter. The russet leaves falling silently in the moonlight, drifting to join the fallen Scottish pine needles, symbolised their immediate future. Soon they would be dropping down on the Barren Mountains, where few trees grew.

They had been trained to the peak of physical and operational fitness. Jens Poulsson was their leader, a lanky, level-headed hillsman, still in his early twenties. He had sat at the same school desk as Claus Helberg.

"I first met Claus when his mother telephoned my mother and asked if he could come around to play. A very small boy in a very large hat appeared. On skis, of course. I think the parents thought we might keep each other out of trouble if we were together," says Poulsson.

At twenty-three, Helberg was heading for the big trouble, with his old schoolmate, after trading in his floppy outsize tam-o-shanter for a parachutist's thick-blocked crash helmet.

Craggily handsome as his native mountains, he has a frosting of grey hair, like the snow caps now. Just over six feet tall, with the mile-eating stride of a born mountaineer, he learned to send Morse at twenty words a minute, in any emergency likely to arise—and he knew twenty-one different ways of killing a German sentry, silently.

Arne Kjelstrup, who had come down the mountain pipeline to a plumbing business in Oslo, treasured a pair of shears, later to save his life. Earlier, perhaps, the western world.

Knut Haugland[1] was generally accepted as second-incommand if Jens Poulsson was killed. The four sweated and fretted as they read and re-read the tattered Norwegian newspapers of ten days or a fortnight before, and saw the empty bunks as others of their number disappeared on unknown missions.

They were kitted up to the moment of take-off; long woollen singlets, two pairs of socks—one long, one pair short —ski boots from Canada—they refused point-blank to accept the British issue—civilian shirts, gaberdines, wind-proof trousers, anaraks (parkas), sunglasses, woollen sweaters, white camouflage smocks, ski-caps and anklets. They had their British battle-dresses. With "Norge" shoulder tabs.

"It was rather amusing about the anklets," recalls Poulsson.[2] "Like the boots, we did not fancy the English issue. Some of the dear old ladies shopping with us in a famous Knightsbridge store would have fainted if they had guessed

---

[1] Now Major Haugland, D.S.O., M.C., living at Hovindviden, Oslo. Was the first man to contact London by radio from the Hardanger Vidda.

[2] Now Major Poulsson, D.S.O., Operations Officer, 1st Division Infantry, Royal Norwegian Army, living with his wife Bergljot, named after one of the ancient Viking queens, and thirteen-year-old daughter, at Baerum, Eiksun 62, Oslo.

that they were rubbing shoulders with desperate saboteurs! We found exactly the skiing anklets we wanted. A man with frost-bitten legs on the Vidda would have been such a handicap that most likely he would have wandered away into a snowstorm like your Captain Oates of the Antarctic, rather than lead his comrades to destruction.

"After our final briefing at Chiltern Court we went back to Scotland to wait. That part of it was the worst. And we thought of poor Einar Skinnarland on his own and became more impatient."

They had hardly settled back at Aviemore when the message which Colonel Wilson had dreaded came through from the lonely man of Rjukan.

There was enough heavy water, ready for shipment from Vemork, to satisfy laboratory demands in Berlin.

The details electrified the War Cabinet and sparked off immediate action.

CHAPTER 3

A Strange Bird Flies

—————————————————————————

THE four men, ghostly in their white camouflage smocks, shook hands with Professor Leif Tronstad on the airfield at Wick.

Twice before they had accepted the suicide pill (death within five seconds), a rubber capsule containing zyankalium.

"Spies in civilian clothes had the pills stitched into the lapels of their suits," explains Claus Helberg. "We had to carry ours in the field-dressing pocket of our battle-dresses. As we were wearing smocks on top we pondered about the chances of reaching the pills in good time if we were unlucky enough to be captured."

Twice in September, 1942, they had roared off into the night, sitting on their parachutes, trying not to think too much, flying high over their own coastline and then slipping down into the nearest valley to avoid German radar stations. And twice they returned to base, stiff, coldly miserable.

Heavy cloud over the Hardanger Vidda had made a drop out of the question.

Somewhere below had been the familiar houses, known from boyhood days, nestling into the cliff faces, friends and neighbours, sleeping, unaware. The anticipation and the tension at the sight of their own mountains had drained away from them, when they returned to Wick and the four engines of the Halifax signed off into silence.

"We were indeed lucky that third time," says Poulsson. Thirty minutes before midnight on October 18th, a moon

34

period, they slid from the bomber, one by one, and landed safely on a mountain side at Fjarfeit in the Sognadal, many glacier-and-lake miles from the Vemork objective.

Six containers and two packages went down with them.

"It was eerie, dropping like ghosts, back to Norway," says Kjelstrup.

"We were miles from the plotted point," explains Poulsson. "But nobody could blame the pilot because of the conditions. We felt lucky that we had not landed in Sweden. Or on top of the Gestapo headquarters in Oslo."

"Some idea of the terrain which greeted us can be judged by the fact that it was two days before we recovered the last of the containers," recollects Helberg. "We buried half the food supply and some equipment in a base depot. At first conditions were favourable," he says. "Patches of snow in the clefts, just a dusting elsewhere. Then we were hit by one of the worst storms I have ever seen in the hills. It was impossible to stand against the wind."

Poulsson, not a man given to exaggeration, tells how their cheeks and chins were soon bleeding. He kept a diary of sorts for London as will be seen from what follows.

The storm died as suddenly as it had begun, leaving fair skiing conditions.

On October 21st the leader of the "Grouse" group wrote: "Claus and I skied with full packs into Haugedal, where I knew there was a hut. We failed to find it before night fell, and heard later that it had been moved. Heavy march back in the dark and mist.

"The other two tried in vain to make radio contact with London. We had no paraffin for our primus stoves, and therefore had to ignore good mountain roads where we knew no wood was to be found. I decided to advance through the Sognadal, because of the birch-woods and huts in which we could spend the night."

Their beards were beginning to grow. None of them had washed properly since leaving Scotland. To freshen themselves they rubbed a handful of snow across their faces and cooled their blistered hands in the same way.

On the fourth day the men moved off.

"We set out on our long march. I hoped that our food, with the strictest rationing, would be sufficient for thirty days. We had been told to make no outside contacts except in the gravest emergency such as one of us becoming dangerously ill.

"Good Norwegian doctors never asked questions when a sick or unconscious man was dumped on their hospital doorstep, particularly if he had bullet wounds. All of us had been carefully examined before we left and the only operation necessary was the pulling of a couple of teeth without the help of a local anaesthetic and carried out by firmly holding the patient down!

"At high altitudes and in bitter cold, no man can be expected to carry a load weighing more than thirty kilos. Our equipment consisted of eight such loads. This meant that in our party of four each man had to make three journeys a day over the same stretch.

"The ground was difficult and rugged; the snow heavy and deep. Men who left the ski-tracks sank up to their knees. It was mild weather, though, and clumps of snow stuck to the bottom of our skis. The lakes, marshes and rivers were not properly covered with ice, and our feet were soaked all the time.

"So each day's march was miserably short. We often advanced only a few kilometres. On the very first day I broke a ski-stick. It was a month before I got a new one."

Other entries in the diary;

"We reached a deserted farm-house at Barunuten where we found meat and flour. We ate our fill for the first time since our arrival. We also found a ski-toboggan."

"This evening (October 30th) we came to Reinar. Now we are getting near to the inhabited places. We are very tired. I have a boil on my left hand and have had to have my arm in a sling. The hard toil on short rations has sapped our strength."

A day's ration consisted of a quarter slab of pemmican (dried reindeer meat) a handful each of groats and flour, four biscuits, a little butter, cheese, sugar and chocolate.

Claus, the smiling scout, who grinned through his weariness, was sent back to the empty farm-house to steal all the food he could find to raise supplies from the danger mark.

Poulsson and Kjelstrup went forward cautiously, to reconnoitre the line of advance and Knut Haugland stayed behind and vented his anger on the unco-operative radio set which could not put him in touch with London.

Poulsson records;

"Claus travelled to Barunuten and back—a distance of fifty miles—under terrible conditions. He proved the old Norwegian saying 'A man who is a man goes on until he can do no more—and then goes twice as far'."

"Arne and I did not do many kilometres. I fell through the ice while crossing a river. It was the second time I had done so. We returned very weary to Reinar where Knut told us that just at the moment when he had made contact with London his accumulator had run out. Our plans had to be altered. Our job depends upon being able to find a new accumulator.

"We reached our operational base at Sandvatn on November 6th completely exhausted but glad to have arrived at our destination. The march had taken fifteen days . . ."

Fifteen back-aching days, loaded and trudging through slush, forcing one foot ahead of the other, plodding onwards and thinking of the good hot meal they knew they would not get at the end.

Claus Helberg swooped down like a petrel from the heights and laboured back with another accumulator, borrowed from the dam-keeper at Møsvatn, who was Einar Skinnarland's brother.

Just before the four saboteurs waddled out, walking carefully, they had been cautioned to keep away from Skinnarland himself.

Jens Poulsson, who thinks fast in an emergency, but writes slowly, scribbled in his diary:

"The first thing we had to do was to get into radio contact

with England. We knew they must be anxious about us. An-
tennae masts of a good size were put up. But again we failed
—this time because the W/T set was damp."

They hoisted the radio mast in a full gale above their hideaway hut. And some, secretly, wept like children, as the roar-
ing wind whipped it over their shoulders or lashed it into
their faces. Tears of sheer exhaustion and frustration and, of
course, hunger.

November 9th: "We made contact with England at last.
After this the radio service went well . . . it is eerie in this
wilderness to listen to a man so far away, at long last. Knut
lay in his sleeping bag, with only his sending hand exposed
over the set."

That was when the newly established radio link-up almost
broke down. London suspected they had been taken by the
Gestapo and that a briefed German telegraphist was at the
transmitter, seeking questions in the code, based, but transposed, upon the words of a Christmas carol known to most
Norwegians.

Haugland sucked his chilblained fingers and stuck them
down into warmth. He rolled over on his back and stared at
the leaking roof.

"They are challenging that last send," he said wearily.
"What in the hell did we see walking down the Strand in the
early hours of January 1st, 1941?"

"Three pink elephants," chorused the other three.

"I wouldn't mind earning myself a hangover there right
now," grumbled the operator, rolling back, coding up and
sending the brief, prefixed message: —

To Colonel. Three repeat three pink elephants.

In his Chiltern Court office, where his bed was only along
the corridor throughout the war years, Colonel Wilson,
worried about the situation in Norway, grunted with satisfaction.

He had instructed any agent in danger to by-pass normal
channels of communication in emergency with the two words
—"To Colonel". It meant that a message sent in this way

landed on his in-tray by day or was delivered to his flat by night, without delay. In fact, within seconds of being received.

Although Wilson was emphatic that the way of sending a message by radio telegraphy could be as individualistic as handwriting, and therefore capable of being identified as genuine as it came over the air to the experienced ear, he had not accepted the opinion in the radio room that the " Grouse " group had been captured and tortured into parting with their memorised code. Working in a centrally-heated London office and 4,500 feet above sea level on the bleak Hardanger Vidda produced very different reactions. He had guessed that Knut Haugland had huddled over his set, with numbed fingers, for days and nights.

The trick question had proved him right.

" The German monitoring mentality could never have cracked so frivolous an exchange," he says.

Yet Wilson had sterner matters spoiling his snatched hours of sleep. Skinnarland's top-priority message had, in the current phrase, caused considerable alarm and despondency, within the War Cabinet.

There were consultations with Combined Operations headquarters with the object of mounting a great attack on the heavy-water plant at Vemork. The plan was made known to Chiltern Court.

"Yes," said Wilson softly into the scrambler telephone. "We have the trail-blazers. You go ahead from your end."

So a special Commando airborne unit was formed. Most of the men were from the Royal Engineers. All were volunteers.

They were given the roughest, toughest and shortest training for a big job in the history of the British Army. First of all, advanced parachute instruction at Ringway, Manchester, then the hurried transfer south, to secret billets near London, where a model of the Norsk Hydro plant had been set up under the supervision of Major Leif Tronstad, in a drill hall, formerly occupied by the local Boy Scouts. The professor, it will be noted, had been "promoted".

They became experts with gelignite and fuses and finally blew up the model with scaled down charges.

None of them had any illusions about the near-suicidal task ahead. In more barrack-room language their instructors hammered home Colonel Wilson's thinking.

"For gliders, Norway is near flipping impossible. You'll be lucky if you only break one leg on landing. This is your lot."

The map ringing the Hardanger Vidda was turned face from the wall and lifted on to the easel.

"Weather. Lousy and unpredictable. Glaciers galore, mountains, marshes, precipices, all tossing unexpected air currents in your faces. Landing strips? None. Flat areas? Few. Any questions?"

They straggled past the map. The briefing continued day by day, and they studied and stared, listened, and wondered.

There were thirty-four of them. Seventeen, like peas in a pod, to each shuddering Horsa Mark I glider, whipped off behind the Halifax bombers from the runway.

The oldest was Sapper Ernest William Bailey of the 9th (Airborne) Field Company, Royal Engineers. He was thirty-one and back from his last leave at Paulsgrove, Hampshire.

The youngest, with a boy's serene indifference to all the scrapes that could be encountered, came from the same unit. He was Sapper Gerald Stanley Williams, son of Mr. and Mrs. David Humphrey Williams of Doncaster, and had just celebrated his eighteenth birthday with a pint too many. His official number was 1948916 and, according to the older men who trained with him, "a proper card and always ready to have a bash".

Seven lucky volunteers fractured ribs, broke shoulder blades, or smashed ankles during the parachute training. One was dragged through a nearby potato patch after the drop from the captive balloon. Vegetables were shed in his wake like a mechanical digger.

The aircrews, seven to each Halifax, had been flying Wellingtons and Whitleys, until they heard part of the news at the dawn muster.

"New job for you. New base. One week's leave. Break off and report to the drafting office."

The security cover story had been that their unusual cross-country training of pin-pointing small objectives in all kinds of weather, and a course of gymnasium work, swimming and running, among other stamina tests, was because of a coming contest against the United States Air Force for a non-existent trophy called the Washington Cup.

When the gliders were wheeled into the hangars at the airfield at Wick, starting point for many strange missions against occupied northern Europe, certain crews had been more than half-way to guessing the truth of their ultimate mission. None of them had ever flown with Horsas riding their tail-flaps.

"Take me back to dear old McGill," said Flight-Lieutenant Arthur Roland Parkinson, twenty-six, B.Sc. graduate of that Montreal University. He came from Lachine, Quebec Province. He is buried at Helleland in south-western Norway.

"I don't fancy the idea of hauling those babes half-way across the world," he confessed to his co-pilot, Gerard Sewell de Gency, aged twenty, from Bushey, Hertfordshire.

When the airborne troops fell in for the final training flights with shoulder flashes and divisonal signs un-picked the R.A.F. officers exchanged significant glances and shrugged. That night, after the day's flying, they drifted to the mess and emptied more than the usual number of tankards.

Next morning their guesses were officially confirmed.

"This is it," said the briefing Wing-Commander, tapping his pointer against a big, blown-up photograph of the Norsk Hydro plant.

"The most important target in the world as of now."

"You shed your gliders here." He turned to a map and traced down the length of a fjord, Mjosvatnet, to flat country on the shore near Finflote.

"A welcome will await you. Some of the Norwegians were dropped back home some days ago for the house-warming."

He went into details about ground-to-air recognition signals and radio-beacon position fixing.

"Don't kid yourself," he warned them. "This is really rugged and in more ways than one. For the purpose of this extremely important operation you'll drop normal identification letters and become just 'A for Apple' and 'B for Bertie'. Let's hope there is never any need for a 'tail-ass Charley' to follow through."

The wisecrack died away in front of the earnest young faces, before it hit the curved roof of the big Nissen hut.

He had doodled all over the big map of Sonderausgabe V 1940, with his stick, as if leading the expedition.

"There's trouble below, all over this wicket. Lots of water and half-frozen, most of it, at this time of the year. Fatal for gliders in any crash landings. Whacking great cliff faces, which throw up crazy air currents. Herds of reindeer may foul up your landing strip. Latest intelligence says no wolves or grizzlies but possibly Germans, waiting with open arms. Firearms!

"The first kite will take off at 1715 hours on the nineteenth, followed fifty-five minutes later by 'B for Bertie'. That's you, Flight-Lieutenant Parkinson. The staggered take-offs will give the enemy radar as big a headache as possible. The Yanks will be flying sorties around the same time. But will be well away from your flight paths.

"This lark is the peak of top secrets and there will be no fighter cover, even if they could stretch their wings that far."

In another building, with armed sentries pacing across the double doors, the airborne troops had listened to the briefing of both British and Norwegian officers, as they looked for the last time at the seven-storeyed plant they had come to know so well—to know and hate.

What the men thought they kept to themselves. Nothing excited them and least of all the knowledge that the failure of the mission could deliver the world to the Nazis.

Most of them came from English, Scottish and Welsh homes but Pilot-officer Norman Arthur Davies, twenty-eight, had come a longer way. Right across the world from Melbourne,

Victoria. The other Australian was Pilot-officer Herbert John Fraser. Same age. But he had left a wife, as well as parents, in Bendigo, Victoria.

They traded looks when the senior officer said briskly and without any hesitation:

"Any man badly wounded in the downhill attack or uphill during the withdrawal to the Swedish frontier, must be given morphine. And left behind."

"What a charming thought," somebody in the back seats had drawled below his breath.

"I'll have that quid off you now," said a more belligerent Scottish voice, as they filed out, back to their quarters. "In case we're paid off in washers or that Swedish money which I don't rightly understand."

They passed the waiting time, each to his feelings and temperament. Some had written carefully worded, shielded letters on the scrubbed tables.

In one nook of the big Nissen the noisy, cursing dart players blamed the fumes from burners, fed with coal and peat, for their failure at the board. Others playing dominoes or cards occasionally rounded on them with mild oaths enjoining them to be quiet.

"Stop tha bloody belly-achin'," said a big Yorkshireman with quiet disgust.

Near one of the stoves Driver Ernest Pendlebury, aged twenty-five, from Wellington, New Zealand, stood with outstretched hands trying to coax some heat as he glanced at a youngster on a truckle bed with a bible propped up in front of him.

Nobody shared their thoughts, but everybody looked up when a spry young Cockney returned from a trip out-of-doors.

"'Appy looking lot of 'eroes," he said with a grin. "Just 'ad a butcher's outside and I can promise you there'll be no bleedin' operations tonight. That ought to cheer you geezers up."

The little Cockney turned out, however, to be a false prophet, for on the dot of 5-15 p.m., by the civilian clocks of nearby Wick, the first Halifax plus Horsa was on the runway and the other lined up at 6-10.

Exactly six hours and twenty-six minutes later radio silence was broken by the first bomber, unheard by the Scottish townsfolk who had listened to the roar of departure.

"*Request course back to base.*"

Fourteen minutes later it signalled tragedy from the air.

"*Glider has dropped into sea.*"

No message was ever passed by "B for Bertie" to any British station.

CHAPTER 4

The Man Who Threw His Voice

"On account of the increased number of cases in which aircraft are used for landing saboteurs, who do serious damage, I order that personnel from sabotage aircraft shall be shot immediately by the first persons who come into contact with them."

Directive from Hitler on October 18th, 1942.

E VERY man who managed a glimpse at the dimmed flarepaths of Wick dropping astern that night knew full well their fate next dawn if taken by the enemy across the North Sea.

Only the seven aircrew of "A for Apple" ever saw their families again.

Five airborne troops lived out a dreary fifty-nine days of captivity without suffering torture and giving nothing away. The others died within twenty-four hours of take-off—some of them horribly, even by Gestapo standards.

The two Halifax bombers, with their trembling charges behind, sped towards the Norwegian coast at different times and altitudes.

So far, so good. The little convoy, upon which so much depended, must have believed in their luck, until they had to wrestle with a new and unlooked for weather front which made course-holding difficult for the pilots, and some men in the gliders air-sick.

Their landfall must have been miles off the charted lane. The Norwegian hills, loaded with ore which bemused the

45

magnetic compass, could not have welcomed them properly, and the gyro-indicators therefore reacted disastrously.

Poulsson, Haugland, Helberg and Kjelstrup had paid many anxious visits to the agreed landing strip, trampling out with slender skis any spot that looked dangerous to a flimsy glider, but the bombers had not come. Back in the hut, Haugland sat crouched over the radio set and said to his leader, "They must have run into trouble and have had to return to base."

The trouble was very much worse than Haugland imagined, for death had come already to many of those involved in "Operation Freshman"—headquarters identification for the ill-fated mission.

As the weather lifted and cleared around the small "Grouse" group, pushing their bone-weary legs into their clammy sleeping-bags, to await yet another day of anxiety, security regulations slammed down in Britain. Relatives of the dead worried for weeks about the fate of their next of kin.[1]

The glider towed by Flight-Lieutenant Parkinson from Canada must have crash-landed about the same time as the parent bomber plunged into a hillside, killing the entire air crew outright.

Besides the graves of Parkinson and his young co-pilot in the village churchyard of Helleland, in south-western Norway, about ten miles inland from the port of Egersund, lie their observer, Flight-Lieutenant Arthur Edwin Thomas, aged thirty-two, from Bexhill, Sussex; his opposite number in the Halifax, Flying-Officer Arnold Haward of Cuddington, Cheshire; Flight-sergeant Albert Buckton of West Hartlepool, County Durham, telegraphist and air gunner; Flight-sergeant George Mercier Edwards, official number 1259259, air gunner and the flight-engineer, Sergeant James Falconer from Edzell, Angus, Scotland, aged twenty.

Only three men from the lost glider were killed on impact. The others were rounded up by German patrols and driven with their dead comrades to the nearby Egersund garrison.

[1] I am indebted to Captain Syvertsen of Forsvarets Krigsgrav-Og, at Frognel-liren, housed in barracks built, ironically, by the German invaders, just out-side Oslo, for help in piecing together for the first time details of the end to a gallant and desperate failure.

There they were shot, without trial, before some of them, stunned by shock, realised what was happening.

The pilot and co-pilot of "A for Apple", interrogated on landing back at Wick, wearily gave the first clues to the fate of the others.

Their aircraft had run into heavy cloud masses about forty miles west of their given landing strip. They had turned back and then the tow and the glider had begun to ice up.

"The tow finally parted. There was nothing we could do for the poor devils spiralling down into the snow."

The glider hit the ground with more force than the other. Only nine men were left alive, four seriously injured. They never knew it, but they were on a snow-lashed mountain peak at Fyljesdal.

The victims of the crash were taken to Stavanger hospital, but not from any motives of mercy. The Gestapo were there and when it was realised that the injured were too ill to be interrogated, the officer in charge gave the doctor present a curt nod and left. It was in this manner that sentence of death was passed and it was carried out medically.[1] The weighted bodies of the victims were later dumped into the sea.

Twenty-four hours after the disaster the German-controlled Oslo radio announced that two British bombers, each towing a glider, had flown in over southern Norway. They had been forced down and the crews were killed to the last man in a fight.

The five survivors from the second glider were transferred, blindfold, to the Grini concentration camp which is thirty miles drive from the shopping centre of Oslo. They were:

Sapper James Frank Blackburn, 9th (Airborne) Field Company, Royal Engineers, aged twenty-eight, married, Isleworth, Middlesex.

[1] Resistance hero Knut Haukelid believes the four were poisoned but Claus Helberg, his fellow saboteur, heard from local sources that the doctor, so-called, had injected air bubbles into their veins and stood by, stop-watch in hand, noting their dying moments.

The whole truth will never be known. The killer was the first man to be claimed by the local Milorg group at the time of the uprising.

Sapper Frank Bonner, his friend, twenty-five.

Lance-corporal Wallis Mahlon Jackson of the same unit, twenty-one. Meanwood, Leeds.

Sapper John Wilfred Walsh, aged twenty-one. Stretford, Lancashire.

Sapper Thomas William White. Gilfach Goch, Glamorgan.

The last man to talk to them before their execution, after fifty-nine days' imprisonment, was a Norwegian, the only prisoner in alley 40 on the second floor of Grini who could speak English fluently. He has asked the writer to respect his anonymity and reveals that when he was arrested for the second time and taken to Grini, the five doomed men had already been lodged there. He himself had been travelling to Malmö and thence to Stockholm, ostensibly on business, but really to arrange for the transmission of information to London. The time came though, as he felt it must, when there was a dawn knock on his door and he was arrested.

He says that the British captives were not ill-treated or tortured. The block commandant, a creature called Kunze, vented his cruelty only upon Norwegian prisoners.

"There are certain experiences that one never forgets," says this eye-witness, "and what happened at Grini, and elsewhere, remains terribly clear to me.

"The one meal of the day was either Berliner soup—hot water with pieces of bread and unpeeled vegetables—or fish and potatoes. He always kicked my platter across the cell and on soup days I went hungry. Other times I could always scrape some fish from the dirty floor.

"I talked with the British airborne troops by means of a ventriloquist's trick we had perfected. There was a grating at the bottom of each cell. When the guards were away, and they disappeared with true Teutonic regularity, if you quietly ran the cold water as cover you could pitch your voice, like playing billiards, until you cannoned into the right place.

"I talked with the five as often as possible, without risking torture for them. They gave nothing away, just names and

COLONEL J. S. WILSON. Not without reason the saboteurs talked about him as "the Scoutmaster" between themselves.

Briefing in a London block of flats—for the dangerous parachute jump into Norway. Three of the men in the photograph made the drop. POULSSON (with the pipe) HELBERG and KJELSTRUP on the right of the reconstructed scene.

numbers. Nothing more. From their voices they seemed mere boys.

"I was arrested on December 11th, what we Norwegians call 'The Devil's birthday'. The British were taken out one February morning and shot. I spoke with them through the grating before they went. They did not know they were about to be executed without trial and were in good spirits. The Germans had told them they were to see a new type of glider."

They were buried in one of two mass graves at Trandum,[1] together with captured British agents, seamen and local patriots, but to-day their names are to be found on the crosses at Vestre Gravlund in the north-western outskirts of the city.

Most of their comrades have a memorial in the Eganes churchyard, half a mile away from the post office at the busy south-western seaport of Stavanger.

The head crosses in that plot called "Z" show how a small group of determined men, from all parts of the world, met their end together.

Alphabetically : —

Lieutenant Alex Allen, aged twenty-four. Hugglescote, Coalville, Leicestershire.

Sapper Ernest William Bailey, aged thirty-one. Paulsgrove, Hampshire.

Driver John Thomas Vernon Belfield, aged twenty-six. Son of Thomas and Eliza Belfield, Longnor, Staffordshire.

Sapper Howell Bevan, aged twenty-two. Bermondsey, London.

Lance-corporal Fred Bray, aged twenty-nine. Edenbridge, Kent.

Lance-corporal Alexander Campbell, aged twenty-four. Grangemouth, Stirlingshire.

Pilot-Officer Norman Davies. Melbourne, Victoria.

Sergeant Peter Doig, aged twenty-five. Won his wings with the 1st Glider Pilot Regiment. Glasgow.

---

[1] When the day of liberation came the Norwegians forced Quisling, the man who added a new word to the English language, to help dig up the graves. He vomited several times when he came across corpses with hands tied behind their backs, sometimes with barbed wire. But the bayonets kept prodding. Then he was legally tried, found guilty of many war crimes, and executed.

Sapper William Thomas Faulkner, aged twenty-two. Hereford.

Pilot-Officer Herbert John Fraser. Bendigo, Victoria.

Sapper Charles Grundy, aged twenty-two. Salford.

Lance-sergeant Fred Healey, aged twenty-nine, husband of Mrs. Thurza Healey, Chester-le-Street, Durham.

Sapper John Glen Vernon Hunter, aged twenty-two. Lennoxtown, Stirlingshire.

Sapper William Jacques, aged thirty. Husband of Mrs. Elizabeth Jacques, Arnold, Nottinghamshire.

Lance-sergeant George Knowles, aged twenty-eight. Husband of Mrs. Lillian Knowles, Bromley, Kent.

Sapper Herbert J. Legate of the 9th (Airborne) Field Company, Royal Engineers. Age and address unknown to Norwegian authorities.

Lieutenant David Alexander Methven, aged twenty. Awarded George Medal.

Sapper Robert Norman, aged twenty-two. Brechin, Angus.

Driver Ernest Pendlebury, Wellington, New Zealand.

Driver George Simkins, aged thirty, husband of Mrs. Bessie Simkins, Romford, Essex.

Sapper Leslie Smallman, Hednesford, Staffordshire.

Sapper James May Stephen, 261st (Airborne) Field Park Company, Royal Engineers. Age and home address unknown.

Staff-sergeant Malcolm Frederick Strathdee of the First Glider Pilot Regiment.

Corporal John George Llewellyn Thomas, Bath, Somerset.

Sapper Gerald Williams, aged eighteen. Son of Mr. and Mrs. David Williams, Doncaster, Yorkshire.

Long before the "Missing—presumed killed" telegrams, with their burdens of personal grief, had been delivered, the War Cabinet had again met to consider the Norway problem. The situation was, if anything, more critical than ever and called for decisive action.

Colonel Wilson told his staff and Professor Tronstad: —

"I've 'phoned Combined Operations our deepest sympathy on this disaster. I suggested we took over the responsibility for the next enterprise and they agreed at once. The War Cabinet has consented. It's now up to us. Up-to-date information indicates that six men, expert skiers and highly-trained, plus the "Grouse" group can do appreciable damage to the high concentration plant. Major Tronstad and I have selected Joachim Rønneberg as the leader. I've spoken to Scotland and told them to tell him to select his team. Intensive training begins tomorrow. A signal has been sent to the advance party to hold their hand. For closer security their code-name has been changed to 'Swallow' as of now."

When he was alone again Wilson studied the large-scale maps of Norway for a long time and found little that was encouraging. There were Germans everywhere. From Narvik in the north to Kristiansand in the south. His opposite numbers in the French and Dutch Sections had a relatively easier task getting their men in and out of occupied territory—and no target like Norsk Hydro to haunt them.

He checked the signal log with the renamed "Grouse" group. The importance of the mission was reflected in the traffic. In one month alone London had sent them fifty-four messages. During this time Knut Haugland had transmitted no less than ninety-five.

At this moment he had nineteen men in Norway, some of them trained in Britain, instructing their countrymen in wireless telegraphy and sabotage under the most dangerous circumstances. One agent was completely unknown to Special Executive Operations, but fed in by air the most valuable information. In the official files the words "Never heard" comes under the ultimate fate column.

He drew his finger down the log of life-and-death on this dismal day.

Captured and working for the enemy, only two. And one had prefixed his first trap message—"Sending under duress" in the agreed key-shift which only the experienced London experts could recognise. He died later in a Gestapo gaol.

The second man escaped back to London through Stockholm.

Wilson had lost two, he reckoned. One, A. M. Vaerum, code-called *Penguin*, died gallantly when he shot it out with German guards on landing. He took several with him.

But the chittering over the air from that bird which had shrunk from a "Grouse" to a "Swallow", Wilson's hungry team on the Hardanger Vidda, was all-important, and Haugland's chilled thumb and forefinger had provided, more than any other transmitting station, the information most needed in Chiltern Court.

The thoughts of Colonel Wilson returned to the report he had prepared for the Cabinet. He had been quite frank about the present situation and past operations and had shown that success and failure had come in about equal measure. Among many factors that worried him was the extent of the death-roll among loyal Norwegians—the bitter fruit garnered by the resistance forces and those who rendered aid from without.

The dilemma, Wilson knew, was understood in top British and Norwegian circles and his activities endorsed so that he had been able to assert in his communication to the Cabinet:

> The threat of reprisals by the Nazis cannot be permitted to justify the cessation of all activities of an aggressive nature. But there is this much to be said in relation to the problem. The use by the enemy of reprisals as a weapon demands that the utmost care be taken in the preparation and planning of every operation that is undertaken, particularly the thorough training of all personnel. . . .
>
> Nothing is of greater importance than the collection of reliable information right up to the last moment of the launching of any enterprise, for this is as vital as the thorough training of personnel, the provision of correct equipment and supplies and, of course, transport.

Wilson had spoken, too, of other factors, and, being a soul-searching and conscientious officer, had bluntly set down what he believed were the reasons for failure. This analysis, in fact, as was intended, was spiked with sign-posts that anyone engaged in the deadly business of resistance work could ignore only at his own peril and that of those who worked with him.

Sparsely populated areas cannot shelter outsiders except for a limited period and it is asking for trouble to expect otherwise. Dependable and loyal Norwegians, who have been returned to their country to carry out specific tasks, tend to regard an Allied landing as fairly imminent and, in some instances, act accordingly.

There is also a tendency to over-rate the loyalty of relatives and former friends by taking them on trust too freely and to under-rate, as the result of months of safety, danger from the enemy's counter-espionage activities.

It is a grave mistake to attempt a combination in any part of two separate objectives. Personnel should never be landed at the same time as arms dumps. No two arms dumps should be landed in the same neighbourhood or separate organisers sent on the same trip. A succession of trips should never be undertaken unless there is absolute certainty that the preceding trip has been achieved without arousing the slightest suspicion. Any boat or craft carrying out an operation should not visit more than one place on the coast during the trip. The closest liaison with other organisations conducting operations on the Norwegian coast is absolutely essential.

Prior arrangements for the reception of personnel or arms, whether by air or otherwise, must be carefully made.

Activity by radio, and on the field, must be limited to what is strictly essential. It is far better for a man to do too little than to attempt too much. And in this connection there is a lesson for those responsible in Britain. It is not advisable that they should expect too much in the way of detailed reports, simply for the purpose of compiling statistics.

At the same time, it must be recognised that details and small things count for a great deal in any subversive and secret organisation and no point is ever too small to be overlooked.

Day-to-day changes are taking place in Norway and

those who have been absent from the country for as short a period as six months are hardly able to appreciate new dangers that have arisen and call for unremitting vigilance.

A tube of toothpaste of British origin could mean the capture and strangulation of a highly-trained agent from a pool whose numbers are limited, while a forged identity card might suddenly become out-of-date as an agent waded ashore on a lonely beach or landed in the snow further inland.

The root cause of the various defeats that have been sustained is the limited population in Norway. Personnel sent into the field from Britain, with tasks connected with the organising and instructing of secret movements or guerilla bands, create an unwonted activity in a very small community. Sooner or later this causes a natural curiosity amongst otherwise well-meaning people. If a man has been known previously in the locality his return is bruited abroad. If he is a stranger, he is open to suspicion. There is conclusive evidence to show that agents from Britain have been regarded as *agents provocateurs*.

Some appreciable time before Colonel Wilson had set down the foregoing, Poulsson, more than ever beset by the nagging difficulties at the hungry, sub-zero post on the wilderness of Hardanger Vidda, made the following note in his diary: "It was terrible to hear of the loss of the Halifax and gliders, especially as the weather here has since become so much better. It is a consolation to know that another attempt is to be made in the next moon period."

Poulsson, and indeed everybody concerned with a mission yet to be fulfilled, would have had little cause for optimism had they known that a large-scale map, with Vemork, Europe's biggest Allied target, ringed in red, had been gleefully snatched from the knee pocket of a dead airborne leader in one of the crashed gliders.

CHAPTER 5

"A Pistol is a Man's Best Friend"

"IF you get your enemy on the ground kick him to death if your boots are your only weapons, but don't ever forget that this is your best friend."

The British instructor waved a pistol beneath their noses at the Special Sabotage Training School No. 3, near Southampton—the base the Nazis called "the Gangster School".

He spun the chambers with a practised thumb and continued the exhortation.

"This is your only friend. The only friend you can rely upon in close combat. Treat him properly and he'll take care of you."

"Maybe the Germans were justified, for once," says the softly spoken, hard-as-nails Knut Haukelid.[1] "The motto at that seminary for saboteurs was simply—*Never give the enemy half a chance*. It was drilled into us day and night."

Colonel Haukelid confesses of his yesterdays that he was a born killer. Of animals, for food in the mountains and for the dangerous thrill of outwitting stampeding herds of reindeer in their protective surroundings, and of Germans, who had debauched his beloved countryside.

His twin sister is the internationally known actress Sigrid Gurie. He too is a personality of many moods and facets.

His closest friends know him as an out-of-doors philosopher,

[1] Now Colonel-Lieutenant Knut Haukelid, D.S.O., M.C., Battalion Commander and Second-in-Command of the Telemark Infantry Regiment at Kongsberg, four hours drive from the scene of his wartime exploits in the Rjukan valley.

in a way, a mystic with muscles. He believes in trolls, the legendary creatures who inhabit the quiet sanctuaries of his native land.

On an express train between Oslo and Kongsberg, over breakfast at bleak eight o'clock he cracked his egg-shell and declared firmly: —

" Quisling and his Nazi cronies could never have held Norway for any length of time. The trolls would have fixed them."

In the early days of 1940, when he was helping to build a new jetty at Narvik, to be used to unload war materials for the Finns, he had already decided, come what may, to give the trolls a helping hand against the encroachment from the south.

" Trolls against Hitler—surely not? "

" Oh, yes. Definitely. The Wehrmacht did not know our mountains. A troll could will a fir cone, a Norwegian fir cone, to fall in a certain spot. It is shaped, and looked just like, a hand grenade, but it is much more powerful. It may be hidden by the snow on a ski track. A clumsy foot—then the avalanche. And another German patrol wiped out."

Haukelid was only twenty-nine when he awoke to a Trondheim dawn, in a friend's house, to find the town already filled with Nazi troops.

There was still a chance. They grabbed their skis and slipped around the back of houses and through the cordons, streaking for the nearest Norwegian volunteer detachment they might find. With a group of students, they managed to board a goods train at the railway junction of Stören, Oslobound.

Not that they intended to travel that far, even if the tracks had not already been blown up by the invaders.

The rallying point, like that of the Scottish Covenanters of old, was deep in the moors. It was Hedmark, a mobilisation centre.

They begged for weapons but there were none to spare. They were waved southward, in the direction of the massed forces of the Germans. At Brandbu their commandeered lorry stopped. They were handed Krag rifles and limited ammunition.

Haukelid and the others, some of them mere boys, fought in the delaying action at Hönefoss.

"In the end the Hun threw in his tanks and it was all over," he recollects. "I took to the hills, where I knew no German could capture me. Yes, it was back to the trolls."

In the summer of 1940, living wild, he had netted enough fish from Lake Langesjöen to sell for preserving and to buy basic stores to carry him through the hard winter ahead. But he hungered for action against the Germans.

When Sverre Midtskau, his old friend, was landed by a Holy Loch-based submarine on the western coast, and contacted him, through a mutual acquaintance, he had left his mountain hideaway and returned to Oslo—and the beginning of his undercover war.

"This," said Sverre, producing a small, yellowish container, "I have disciplined myself into thinking about as ' my butter box'—simply because I talk in my sleep! "

Haukelid had stared down at the simple transmitter.

"It doesn't look much," he said.

"Strong enough to reach London—if we're lucky."

They worked to earn enough money to keep alive and to buy 'bus tickets to the outer woods of Oslo, where they took their tiny set in the dark hours, skirting German barricades, road-blocks, and reliving boyhood adventures they had once shared together.

The set, primitive forerunner of many, could only be worked from the mains and the small hut, in which they slept out the soaking nights, possessed no such power. It meant chancy climbs up selected lamp standards, well away from German sentries or roving patrols.

There could have been no trolls to help so near the big city. Despite all their efforts, they were never able to make radio contact. Panting down from a dizzy height Haukelid would gasp many times: —

"Did they hear us? "

"No! Nothing."

"What, again? "

" And we must move. Two hours of solid transmission from the same area in three nights. The Nazis' radio-location vans

will be pin-pointing us. Come on. We'd better get out
of it."

They left the set in another birch hut, beneath the earth,
and carefully covered by canvas, and a layer of branches, and
battled back into Oslo against the snow. By the time they had
returned there was little time left for sleep.

Late that autumn Sverre was summoned back to Britain,
by a message passed through many lips and hands. He went
by fishing smack through the skerries, and the net of German
patrol craft from Vestlandet.

He came back, of course, by solitary drifting parachute.
The first Haukelid and his small group knew of his safe
landfall in Britain was the changed preamble to the British
Broadcasting Corporation's news-cast.

Instead of—"This is London with news in Norwegian," it
had become—"This is London with a news message in Norwegian."

Sverre Midtskau landed unscathed, but his new and powerful radio set was smashed to pieces. Haukelid was one of
many who had trampled out a landing patch and marked
the area with branches of the small trees they had had to dig
from under the fresh snow.

His friend Sverre had touched down, blind, and had been
dragged along by the wind, fifty miles from the plotted point.

Yet he had burst into their shelter hut, late the next night,
bubbling with fresh information, loaded down with cigarettes,
bottles of whisky and copies of *The Times,* only two days
old.

"We began to feel we were getting ahead of the game,"
says Colonel Haukelid, borrowing an Americanism. "But we
did a very stupid thing. We spread the newspapers out on
the sidewalk of one of the main squares in Oslo. It stopped
the traffic all right, but it also stepped up Gestapo activity in
the area."

When his friend was taken by the Gestapo, along with
another Resistance hero, Max Manus, D.S.O., M.C. and Bar,
who escaped by jumping out of a train, Haukelid had moved
north to Trondheim. He was working at the expanding U-
boat base there by day and transmitting what he had learned

to Britain by night. The Trondheim cell at that time was the most active in Norway, except for the bigger group in Oslo.

The Gestapo had planned the swoop at Oslo with methodical care but Haukelid escaped the dragnet and twice returned to the capital before arrangements were made for a transfer to Britain and training. He had known all about the "Linge" Company and, in his determined fashion, he had allowed few days to pass before he was shaking hands with his old friends. Captain Linge impressed him greatly, but he was not to know the officer for long. Three weeks later Linge died in the Maaloy raid.

Haukelid himself was drafted to the training camp near Southampton, where he found a group of young Norwegians from every walk of life.

With them he had learned how to handle small arms and explosives properly, to force locks and blow open safes. From there he graduated to Aviemore in the mountains, onwards to Ringway, Manchester, to learn how to parachute—in the dark.

But for what he described as "the most stupidly frustrating accident of my life," he would have jumped with the "Grouse" group. During a field exercise, however, he stumbled with a loaded revolver in his hand and a bullet went through his foot. While in hospital he had heard that he had been left behind.

On his discharge, he received better news from Professor Tronstad.

"I was literally hopping mad. A pistol had certainly not been my best friend, but then I learned that a reinforcement group, code-named "Gunnerside", had been formed and that I was one of the chosen six."

Six plus four, with Einar Skinnarland, in his eyrie overlooking the plant, making up Colonel Wilson's team of the most determined eleven ever to move into some foreign field.

Haukelid's companions in the "Gunnerside" group were:

Joachim Rønneberg, already named as leader; Kasper Idland. (Decorated by Britain and his own country. Now living at 81, Tower-street, Huntington, New York.); Fredrik

Kayser; Birger Stronsheim and Hans Storhaug, M.M. ("The Chicken"[1]).

At Chiltern Court, Colonel Wilson began an earnest discussion with colleagues and assistants into the plans for sending over the new group known as "Gunnerside". Absolute secrecy, he said, was imperative as he explained that the men were to be moved south for final training on the model of the Norsk plant reconstructed from information and photographs provided by Professor Jomar Brun. (Formerly chief engineer there. He escaped to London, via Stockholm, and was able to provide vital information to the British authorities. He was awarded an O.B.E. later and is now at the Department of Industrial Electro-Chemistry at the Institute of Technology, Trondheim.)

Colonel Wilson said he was anxious that the equipment and supplies should be out of the top drawer and that arrangements with the Air Section for the dropping of the group over Norway should be perfected to the last detail. Present at this conference was the leader of the group, Joachim Rønneberg (now a broadcasting executive at Alesund and who once spent part of a belated honeymoon at Colonel Wilson's home near Maidstone). During the talk Rønneberg picked up a Lee-Enfield, examined it in the manner of a man who knew a rifle when he saw it, and then said, "I'd rather have a Krag."

"Don't you know there's a war on?" somebody asked him.

When the "Gunnerside" group got together they talked of the task that lay ahead. They reckoned they would need a little luck to pull off the job at the plant and Haukelid assured them that the trolls would help.

But as time went on a succession of postponements brought disappointment. Waiting was indeed a miserable and nerve-wracking business.

[1] Storhaug was caught, red-handed, gutting a pheasant by an angry Scottish gamekeeper. He took evasive action and slipped away but the gamekeeper went down to headquarters and complained of the incident.

"Can you positively identify this man?" asked the duty officer.

"Aye that I can," was the reply. "He had a great ruddy beak and looked like a chicken!"

Storhaug escaped the consequences, for what they were, but ever afterwards he became known as "The Chicken".

They had been taken to a requisitioned mansion outside Cambridge, near another airfield of secret departures, and had been there almost three months. Throughout the moon periods they had received, each day, the tantalising message thrice repeated:

"No operation to-night. No operation to-night. No operation to-night."

The deplorable winter of 1942-43 in southern Norway kept them earthbound and exasperated. For Haukelid, in particular, who thought about the half-starved "Grouse" group he had just missed joining, the waiting had been the most irksome. He was to have another major disappointment in January, 1943, before finally touching down on his happy, reindeer hunting grounds of the Hardanger Vidda.

During the first month of the year "No operations to-night" was, for everybody, gloriously reversed and Professor Tronstad arrived at the rain-lashed airfield hut to shake hands with the group and wish them the best of luck.

As the saboteurs clambered into the aircraft, each made certain that the pills, which would defeat the Gestapo, were easily available. But for all the precautions and high hopes, the weather triumphed that night and made the drop impossible.

The four-engined bomber with the R.A.F. roundels pulsed back, defeated, to base, after frantic waves of welcome from Norwegians below, even the sight of Norwegian dogs racing along the snow-bound roads, snapping at the shadow thrown by the big aircraft.

The four engines had laboured in vain for almost the same number of hours, searching through snow cloud for the markers on the Hardanger Vidda. For minutes on end the heart-beats of the men echoed the noise from the wings. Somewhere below was their homeland.

They had turned away to the west again, the six most miserable Allied saboteurs ever sent on any abortive mission.

"We were frozen, fed-up and very far from home," recalls "The Chicken".

"We wanted to drop," says Rønneberg. "But the pilot would have none of it."

Soon after their return, and at their own request, the six had been moved to the isolation of a little stone hut, with white-framed windows staring towards Mull, just outside Oban, to wait for the next full moon.

"Away from the fleshpots of London's West-end," remembers Haukelid. "We were trained to the limit of peak physical fitness, and knew we had to stay that way to keep alive."

They fished, tramped the moors, and shot game.

"The waiting, of course, was the worst of it," says Haukelid. "Before I arrived in Britain I was something of the well-meaning amateur. Weeks, months had passed. I was suddenly a trained man, specialising in sabotage, but with nowhere to go."

He had protested, vehemently, when Colonel Wilson and Professor Tronstad had insisted he should find his way with the others into Sweden, after the success—or failure—of the Vemork adventure. It was intended, of course, that they should return to London.

Wilson had known that, once there, the saboteurs would not want to leave their country again. He listened, and not without sympathy, to Haukelid's angry protests.

"I shall not come back to Britain," he declared. "I want to go back into the hills after we have tackled the big job. I can promise you that those louts will never find us. When the time comes we'll organise the final uprising in Telemark and it will save many lives and the destruction of property."

Haukelid, speaking rapidly in Norwegian, then tried to persuade Professor Tronstad to endorse his plea but without success. He was a very angry man.

February had arrived and the six men had come south again, somewhat nervy and keenly aware that their comrades on the Hardanger Vidda had been living for the past five months like hunted, hungry animals. It was like a betrayal not to be with them.

Not any time did they ever become reconciled to the delay, but they had a much shorter wait than on the first occasion and once more Professor Tronstad came down to the airfield to wish them good fortune in their attempt to destroy the great plant he had helped to create.

On the evening of February 16th, 1943, the plane took off in the face of pelting rain. Over Norway it was crisp, cold and moonlit and at midnight the "Gunnerside" group finally parachuted down to the frozen surface of Lake Skryken, thirty miles north-west of where their pinched and hungry comrades were holed up.

At almost the last minute the drop point had been switched to a place well away from the "Swallow" base, following a warning against any aerial activity near to the Rjukan valley.

Knut Haukelid had almost taken one of the British aircrew with him.

"I was the last of our group to go," he says. "When I prepared for the moment of no return I found that the line fastening my parachute to the aircraft was also wound around this dispatcher's body in such a way that we would have crashed to our deaths together. I gave him a mighty heave to the other side of the hole and went out from a standing position. There was no time to sit down."

Like the others, Haukelid had had no illusions about what might await them. The Germans were aware of the presence of saboteurs in the mountains and that the plant at Vemork was their objective. The tell-tale map in Gestapo hands had told them that much and Einar Skinnarland had relayed news of this development to London.

Consequently, the guard at the factory had been strengthened and the garrison at Rjukan doubled. Josef Terboven, the Reichskimmisar, and the Commander-in-Chief for Norway, Colonel-General von Falkenhorst, had personally studied the defences of the valley. Local Norwegians had been arrested in reprisal raids.

All this had immeasurably increased the danger ahead for Fenrik Joachim Rønneberg and the others and they realised on landing just how tenuous their chances were of avoiding discovery.

They had baled out awkwardly at 1,000 feet, hit in the face by a searing ice-laced wind, not quite sure of exactly where they were going. Knut Haukelid, cursing, as only he can curse, almost a non-starter.

"With," he quipped, "a British jockey almost on my back. One who didn't know the form."

Rønneberg's report, jotted down during one of the worst snow-storms ever to hit the Hardanger Vidda, fills in the dramatic details in black against the stark whiteness.

"February 16th. At midnight, precisely, my party of six landed safely on Norwegian soil. We did not kiss the ground. We were much too busy. A package containing four vital rucksacks was dragged some distance across the snows by a wind-bellied parachute, to land in one of the many open ice-cracks. It was salvaged, after a time. One sleeping-bag and two rucksacks were somewhat damaged. Otherwise all gear of use against the enemy retrieved."

They had worked through the bitter morning, for four hours, re-packing equipment from the dropped containers for the advance, burying the remainder, marked with stakes in the snow.

By the time they had finished their toil the driving snows had covered all signs of the landings and digging. They had slept, warily, in the unoccupied summer hunting lodge, which had been pin-pointed for them. It was unheated. Their eyelids were frosted together when they had reluctantly blinked themselves awake.

Rønneberg wrote: "February 18th. A snow-storm of great violence burst upon us. It was impossible to venture out of doors. All of us felt ill because of the change of climate and two had bad colds."

"February 19th. Clear skies. But the storm continues. We made an attempt to reach the depot to fetch food, but had to give up for fear of losing our way. During the night the chimney-pot was blown off the hunting lodge."

"February 20th. Clear skies. Less wind. But still the driving snow. We made another attempt to find food, but the storm had so changed the landscape that even our big stakes were hidden. After three hours the attempt was abandoned. We made a final try the same afternoon and at length found a container."

"February 21st. The snow-storm raged with renewed fury. Visibility was nil. We were filled with a great weariness and

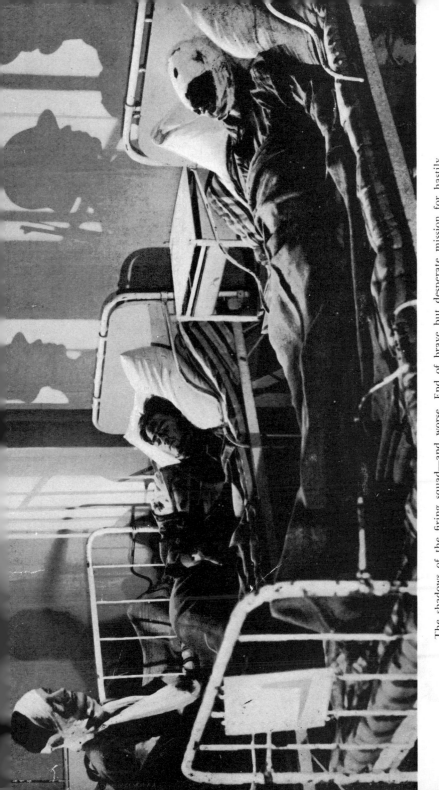

The shadows of the firing squad—and worse. End of brave but desperate mission for hastily trained British Commandos.

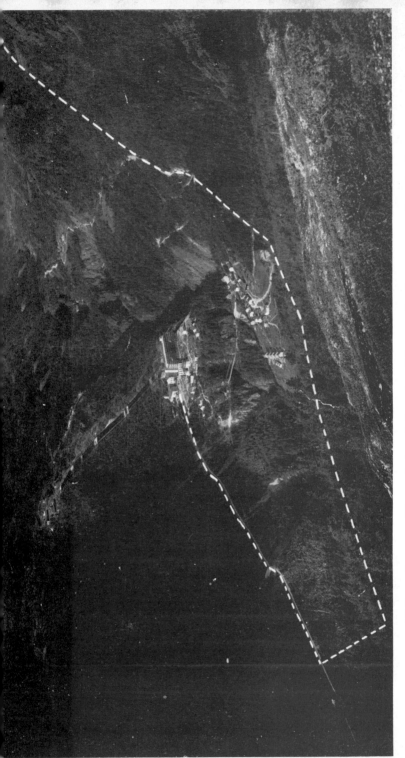

This was the target. The marked track from the wild mountains down, across and up the deep ravine defeated the Nazi belief that Norsk Hydro was impenetrable.

lassitude and the two men who had been suffering from colds were now seriously ill."

"February 22nd. The storm has, at last, blown itself to a standstill. The weather has turned fine. We are preparing to leave at noon."

The saboteurs were a sorry sight. Their lips were blackened and blistered and their half-bearded faces blood encrusted. They had landed enough explosive to demolish both the heavy-water installation and the adjacent machinery, although Professor Tronstad had said that the destruction of the first named would amply fulfil the purpose of the mission. Six days of fearsome storm had almost engendered a hatred for their beloved country and had sapped their strength, despite the rigour of the training they had undergone for months on end. Too much time had been lost already and Joachim Rønneberg promptly decided to bury part of the explosives and thus lighten the load they would all have to carry as they skied to the base for the link-up with Poulsson, Helberg, Kjelstrup, Haugland and, later, with Skinnarland.

They still carried sufficient explosives for the main task and food to share with their comrades on Hardanger Vidda. There, at the base, the men were in a bad way. During the long dispiriting wait for reinforcements, everybody but Poulsson had gone down with sickness and fever, due largely to malnutrition. The base was so short of food that they had been reduced to eating the moss which keeps reindeer half-alive in the bad months. Poulsson went out every day in search of game, but could find none and to make matters worse the stock of dry wood came to an end.

One day Poulsson trudged across the snow, found a family hut, and broke down the door. There was no wood inside but he found a rotting turnip and a bottle of fish oil. He could not resist a taste of each before taking his finds back to share with his companions. Poulsson's nightly craving was for a cigarette and the scanty bedding was less of a trial to him than to others, especially Kjelstrup who, on one occasion, had to be levered in his sleeping bag from the wall of the hut. There was so little heat in his body that he had frozen to the wood!

E

Nevertheless, the men realised how much depended on their staying alive and did what they could to fend for themselves, even to eating moss. Oddly enough Helberg put on weight, the result of a swollen stomach from sheer malnutrition. From London they received splendid encouragement from Colonel Wilson and they saw to it that the accumulator of the transmitter remained charged. It was no mean feat.

On the day that mattered Helberg and Kjelstrup had slowly heaved themselves up the highest point from their hut and stood there utterly exhausted. They had made the trip so many times that it had become a torture. Neither spoke but just grunted and pointed with ski sticks. They had not yet run out of humour, though, and there was a friendly struggle for possession of their only telescope (made in Glasgow) with which to scan the wastes of the Hardanger Vidda, truly translated as the Barren Mountains.

Nothing moved anywhere—certainly not the "Gunnerside" group which London had said was on the way to the base. It seemed like doing violence to sanity to continue to search and both men turned away without saying a word.

Behind them, though, they heard Knut Haukelid's pretence at a cough and their hands went to their holsters. Starved men are not notably quick on the draw and they would have been dead before they had their guns in their hands if an enemy, rather than a friend, had come up on them in this way. When they turned. Haukelid faced them gun in hand, for he, too, had been drilled in Britain not to believe anything he heard and only half of what could be seen.

Haukelid had been sent on ahead by Rønneberg because he knew the Rjukan valley men better than the others. When he first caught sight of Helberg and Kjelstrup he couldn't be certain who they were. They certainly didn't look strikingly like anybody he knew and in less dangerous circumstances they could have drifted past him without getting a second glance. Haukelid crept the last two hundred yards after eyeing them through field-glasses. There seemed something familiar about them but he couldn't be certain and that worried him.

When they turned and faced him he recognised them despite their yellow faces and Kjelstrup's red beard.

"I was about to say, 'Dr. Livingstone, I presume'," recalls Haukelid, "but I saw how ill they looked and a joke, as badly battered as that one, seemed out of place. We just shook hands but it was a great moment."

Helberg says that Haukelid suddenly appeared like a man from another world but he cannot remember an occasion when he was more glad to meet a friend. It wasn't the food so much, and suddenly finding himself in the midst of plenty when they had all returned to the hut at Svensbu, but the feeling that the team had now been made complete—like the forging of a strong chain.

In the crowded hut, with everybody talking at once, and supplies of meat, dehydrated fruits and vegetables, chocolate and cigarettes being poured out of rucksacks by the new-comers, the peril that everyone faced was forgotten for the moment. Poulsson felt guilty about not being able to play host, like every good Norwegian, but he enjoyed the cigarettes and being a true lover of tobacco began to chain smoke.

They slept in cramped positions that night—but they had all slept with easier minds. Next morning Haukelid read out a message from London about future organisation in the province of Telemark, something which had become almost an obsession with him. While preparing for sabotage, his thinking had always been projected into the far future, when his country was freed.

The briefing had been printed on rice paper, which was easy to swallow in the event of arrest. He had been about to crumple it up and toss it into the spluttering, spitting green wood fire in the stove.

"Hey!" Knut Haugland had stayed him. "Is that edible?"

"Could be, I suppose. A bit indigestible."

"Hand over. We don't waste any kind of food here."

Haugland had solemnly munched away as the long delayed attack on the heavy-water plant had been discussed in detail by ten determined men.

Einar Skinnarland, the eleventh man of the mountains, had been pumping information into the uplands in perilous sallies, as his dam, ironically, had kept the factory supplied with the necessary power. The factory was in the ravine, where the sun never shone in five winter months, and the workers needed a German-supervised ski-lift into the surrounding hills to catch their share of its rays. Sometimes, Skinnarland had smuggled the "Swallow" group home-cooked food, baked or stewed, because of the quantity, behind his locked kitchen door. Always, he had added a few additional crumbs of information to make the task of the assault party easier.

That February morning of 1943 the ten in the hut, like desperate, bearded gamblers, had considered his latest bulletin. They had pooled their questions and there were exactly thirty of them.

Claus Helberg smiled that shy grin of his.

"Somebody loan me a bit of ski-wax. And I'll dip down and get the answers."

CHAPTER 6

Saboteurs are not for the Taking

CLAUS HELBERG, aged twenty-three, who had flown to London from Stockholm a year before and had returned to his country a man much older in experience and wariness, had never revealed to his comrades the names of the men and women upon whom he relied for information as to what was happening in the valley of his birth.

The reason for this secrecy was the knowledge that when the Gestapo got to work on suspects they knew how to make them talk. Victims were "scientifically" interrogated under a blaze of fierce light, and if they could not be broken down in this way, they had a few of their finger-nails wrenched out as a preliminary to other unspeakable tortures.

So it was that on this morning of February 25th, when Helberg sneaked down to the valley that had seen happier days, many of those he had known since early boyhood turned away without acknowledging him and for this he was thankful. Everybody lived under the shadow of reprisal and none understood this better than the saboteur.

Helberg's mission, however, was not simply to convince sharp eyes that he was not worth a second glance and, as the day wore on, he made certain of meeting neighbours and old friends who could tell him all that he wanted to know.

During his absence the others decided to move nearer to Vemork—to a point from which they could commence operations. They had shut down on all radio contact with London as the attempt was to be made on Sunday night. Helberg knew of this arrangement and found them at a summer hut in the

69

Fjösbudal two days later. It was then Saturday. He had secured the information that was required and his comrades then began to harry him with questions as to its accuracy and the sources from which it had come. He thoroughly understood their anxiety and assured them they need have no doubt about the reliability of all he had told them.

"Don't forget," he reminded them, "I'll be coming along too."

Helberg had yet another job to do. After a meal and a rest, he left the others, still discussing the news he had brought back, to make a reconnaisance of the approaches and site of the Norsk Hydro—the closest ever made since the Nazi invasion.

Four hours later, they were that close to the target, Helberg was back again with a plan that appeared to make nonsense of the enemy's reliance on the natural defences that guarded the approaches to the heavy-water plant.

He cleared the table and brought a large-scale map of the area. It had been cheekily purchased, practically beneath the nose of a window-shopping German officer, and then marked and identified at the house of a friend.

Ten men stared down at their future, in the dim blue pattern of small lakes of grotesque shapes, swirls of hills, and, most important of all, the great black gash slashed by the Maan to the sea.

Helberg sucked a blistered thumb, gingerly pressed it on the map, and with his index finger made a measure to indicate each point.

"The suspension bridge is seventy-five feet long and it spans the ravine gorged out by the river; perpendicular sides to the river bed, as you all know. That's where they expect the attack to come.

"And that," he grinned, "would be like committing suicide."

"Why?"

"There are always two sentries on patrol from end to end. They could trigger off the searchlights, and alert the machine-guns mounted on the factory roof, before we were half-way across. Their alarm would bring out patrols and more flood-lighting down the Rjukan road, if there was anybody left to retreat.

"If a battalion had attempted to storm that bridge a massacre would be the result. Yet, I think I can put my finger on the weak spot. Here! "

He traced down the map to half-way between Vemork and Rjukan.

"As a boy I have crossed the Maan many times just below that bend at this season. Remember, Jens? "

The leader of the "Swallow" group nodded.

"Yes, I remember. I fished you out a couple of times."

"This year the ice is better, firmer than usual."

"But it gives them so many more miles to spot us," protested one of them.

"We've got to get in there. Undetected," said Rønneberg. "It doesn't matter a damn how far round the houses we have to go."

"And round the houses it will be," answered their scout. "Look! "

Poulsson, Rønneberg, Haukelid and the others watched as he carried his mountain trail through a gap in the fir forest, from the uplands to the lowlands, heading away from their objective, Norsk Hydro, elbow-bending around the inhabited area, a scattering of cliff-clinging timber houses at Vaaer, to his chosen spot.

"We could dump our skis and rucksacks here," Helberg explained, stabbing a point above the departure side of the ravine. "Then we go over the precipice, across the river—and up the other side. Nobody in their right minds would think it possible. But it just is. We follow the railway line on the far side and hit the plant through the back door."

"What about this block bridge below Vaaer? We could run into it there once the alarm is raised? " he was asked.

"We avoid it by going back the way we came as far as the dump. We pick up the gear and take the funicular track into the uplands. Means no ski tracks for them to follow."

"Means a helluva lot of hard climbing, about 1,500 feet from the Rjukan road to the first peak."

"Why not leave by the suspension bridge? "

"And have the guards on our heels?"

In the hut at Fjösbudal they calmly discussed the alternative routes of attack and withdrawal for a long time. They might have been talking about a peacetime ramble instead of a dangerous cross-country climb in the dark with a life-or-death climax. They had come a long way. All they wanted to do was to finish their task quickly and escape.

The Helberg plan adopted, with minor variations, Poulsson and Rønneberg drew up the final operational order:

Intelligence: Fifteen Germans in the hut-barracks between the machine-room and the electrolysis plant. Change of guard at 1800-2000 hours etc. Normally, two Germans on the bridge. During an alarm, three patrols inside the factory area and flood-lighting on the road between Vemork and Vaaer. Normally, only two Norwegian guards inside the factory area at night, plus one at the main gates and one at the penstocks. All doors into the electrolysis factory locked, except one which opens into the yard . . .

"Only fifteen Germans for the most vital target in Norway. They must be mad," said Poulsson.

The Plan: From the advance position at the power-line cutting the following will be brought up. Arms, explosives, a little food. Helberg to lead the way down to the river and up to the railway track. No camouflage suits to be worn over uniforms. Advance to the position of attack some 500 metres from the fence. The covering party, led by Haukelid, to advance ahead along the track, followed closely by the demolition party, which the "Gunnerside" leader will lead himself. The position for attack will be occupied before midnight in order to be able to see when the relieved guards return to barracks. According to information received from sketches and photographs, we have chosen the gate by a store-shed, some ten metres lower than the railway gates, as being best suited for the withdrawal and as providing best cover for the attack. The attack will begin at 0030 hours.

Covering Party: To cut an opening in the fence. To get into position so that any interference by German guards, in the event of an alarm, is totally suppressed. If all remains quiet, to stay in position until the explosion is heard or until

other orders are received from the demolition party leader.
The commander of the covering party to use his own judg-
ment if necessary. If the alarm is sounded during the advance
into the factory grounds, the covering party to attack the
guard immediately. When the explosion is heard, it may be
assumed that the demolition party is already outside the
factory grounds, and the order is to be given for withdrawal.
The password is—" Piccadilly? "—" Leicester Square! "

Demolition Party: To destroy the high-concentration plant
in the cellar of the electrolysis factory. At the precise moment
when the covering party either take up their positions or go
into action, the demolition party will advance to the cellar
door. One man, armed with a tommy-gun, takes up a position
covering the main entrance. Those carrying out the actual
demolition to be covered by one man with a tommy-gun and
one man with a ·45 pistol. An attempt will first be made to
force the cellar door—failing that, the door to the ground
floor. As a last resort the cable-tunnel is to be used. If fighting
begins before the plant is reached, the covering party will,
if necessary, take over the placing of the explosives. Should
anything happen to the leader, or the plans go awry, all are
to act on their own initiative in order to carry out the operation. Any workmen or guards found will be treated as the
situation demands. If possible, no reserve charges will be left
behind in the factory. It is forbidden for members of either
party to use torches or other lights during the advance or
withdrawal. Arms are to be carried ready for use, but are not
to be loaded until necessary, so that no accidental shot raises
an alarm. *If any man is about to be taken prisoner, he under-
takes to end his own life.*

They sat around, just waiting. Some of them smoked,
Poulsson furiously of course. Knut Haugland tinkered with
his mute radio set and Claus Helberg pulled through his
white-painted tommy-gun time after time. A metallic glint
from a snow background could have meant the violent end
of a dream which had begun in Whitehall, S.W.1.

They squinted down pistol barrels they had oiled and
checked the hand grenades they would take with them.

Unlike so many thousands of men at war they had no

letters from home to read and re-read and no family photographs to study. At one time or another they all thought about
that last line in the operational orders.

Knut Haukelid spotted the strangers first. He was sitting
outside the hut with Helberg, who was thinking of any possible snags on the route to which he had committed his comrades. He knew, or believed he knew, the area to his ski tips
Nevertheless, he was worried. Haukelid jerked him out of
his concentration.

"Oh, no," he said dispiritedly, "look!"

Labouring up the hill, headed towards the summer hut adjacent to their own, were two young men and two young
women.

"From Rjukan, I bet. And at this time of the year I wager
they have told their parents that they're off, separately, to do
some shopping in Oslo."

The saboteurs let them go indoors and then surrounded the
shanty, only one tommy-gun between them.

"You will have to stay indoors until Sunday evening,"
ordered the bearded Poulsson, trying not to smile.

"That will be no great hardship," answered one of the girls,
with a slow-motion wink.

"They accepted the situation gracefully," recalls Haukelid,
"and were certainly astonished to find Norwegian soldiers in
the middle of occupied southern Norway in February, 1943.
We had removed the 'Linge' Company shoulder-tabs but
wore British battle-dress, with rank markings. They were
curious but we told them nothing and turned the key in the
door. I would have liked to have talked to them about the
occupation and would probably have discovered mutual
friends in the Rjukan area."

The group then went back to weapon-cleaning, to odd jobs
that needed to be done and to thinking of the hundred-to-one
chance they were to take.

At exactly eight o'clock that Sunday night they set off from
the hut at Fjösbudal, leaving Knut Haugland behind, to
transmit the news—good or bad—to London.

Einar Skinnarland, who had been told of the plans, was the
stop-gap contact over the air. Haugland kept a Krag rifle

beside his set and Skinnarland listened for the sound of an explosion after midnight.

They dumped everything of foreign origin before they buckled on their skis and moved off.

"The first five or six hundred yards down the mountain-side were very steep, and we went at a good pace," says Hauke-lid. "Half-way down we sighted our objective for the first time, below us on the other side. The great seven-storey factory building bulked large on the landscape, although it lay between mountains some three thousand feet high. It was blowing fairly hard, but nevertheless the hum of the machinery came up to us through the ravine.

"We understood then why the Germans were content to keep so small a guard there. The colossus lay like a medieval castle, built in the most inaccessible place, protected by pre-cipices and river."

Nevertheless, although the group believed that the chink in the enemy's defences had been discovered, a fresh peril had been added to the hazards of the mission. Helberg had discovered that earlier on that crucial day large numbers of German troops had been moved into the Møsvatn area. The weather at the start was overcast and mild except for a strong wind. Later the saboteurs found it impossible to use their skis and the approach to the Møsvatn road had to be made on foot. Along the route of the telephone line they entered difficult and steep country into which they sank up to their waists. When they reached the Møsvatn road the knowledge of the presence of German troops near by had everybody on edge but they had to stick to it if they were to reach their objective in reasonable time.

At Vaaer bridge they had to dive for cover when they sighted two 'buses coming up the road with the night shift from Rjukan. Nobody guessed their presence, though, and little time was lost before they were again following the road to the power-line cutting. It had begun to thaw and the road was covered with ice and when they reached the cutting they hid their skis and rucksacks and at 10 p.m. began the steep and slippery descent to the river. There, they found the ice about to break up and the snow-bridge by which they would have to cross aswim with water. They got over and then began the climb up the face of sheer rock for about 150 metres to the Vemork railway line. It was perilous going but they made it safely and hurried along the track until they reached the gate of the factory. Carried on the strong westerly breeze came the faint humming note of machinery.

It was a moonless night but they could see the vista of the rail track and the outline of the factory itself. The saboteurs found a snow-covered hut and waited there for the arrival of the relief guard coming up from the bridge. Most of them were soaked to the waist and badly needed a cigarette, but smoking was out of the question. They had brought some food with them and this they ate slowly, but without much relish.

At the half hour past midnight they watched the guard go by and then Rønneberg reminded his comrades of what was expected of them. They left the hut, stole silently past the great storage sheds, and within a few seconds were standing, shivering with cold, in front of a gate twelve feet wide. The padlock looked inadequate and so did the thin chain to which it was attached. Only this, and a handful of Nazi sentries, stood between these nine men and a coup that had been two years in the planning and had imposed suffering and death.

They knew that the decisive moment had come for them and many others. If they succeeded there would be no atomic bombs shattering Britain later that year—if they failed and were trapped—then they had to seek death quickly and inevitably. Saboteurs were not for the taking.

CHAPTER 7

Within the Gates

o the nine Norwegians the sound of the padlock chain
parting as the armourer's shears bit into it sounded like
a shot that echoed down the length of the Rjukan
valley. They could see, only too plainly, the torches of the
Nazi sentries flickering from the suspension bridge a few yards
away to the right and it seemed impossible for the enemy to
remain unaware that saboteurs were breaking into the Norsk
Hydro.

But sound can be magnified to the ratio of tension and
what the men really heard was nothing more than a discreet
snip, as Arne Kjelstrup, peace-time master plumber from
Oslo, realised when he clutched the padlock and chain in one
hand and slipped the shears back into his pocket with the
other. It had been a simple little job and no trouble at
all.

With the gate now open the saboteurs slipped inside and
those assigned to covering the operation (Haukelid, Helberg,
Poulsson, Kjelstrup and Storhaug) took up temporary positions. The others, who formed the demolition crew (Rønneberg, Kayser, Stronsheim and Idland), went forward and yet
another gate, a few metres ahead, was quickly dealt with.
Rønneberg, who led the way, stopped and listened but heard
nothing. The black-out of the factory was poor and chinks of
light showed in an uneven pattern.

Although the moon was absent, it was a clear night and
the sky spangled with stars. Rønneberg felt some amazement
at the ease of their progress so far—for they were now within

the shadows of the Norsk Hydro—the plant that the Nazis believed invulnerable to any attack by land. Inside, into great containers that would soon be shipped to Hamburg, dripped the heavy water—deuterium oxide without which no German physicist could even dream of an atom bomb.

Rønneberg gave the signal for the covering party to advance towards the hut they knew was occupied by the German guard; at the same time the demolition crew moved towards the door of the cellar which was to provide them with an entry to the factory itself.

Hereabouts some of the men began to throw up and the sickness was not due wholly to the accumulation of anxieties but also to the rigours they had undergone that night and many days and nights before, particularly the original group who had suffered cold and hunger for too long. Without exception, every man had a rasping cough. They were troubled too by a feeling that the British battle-dress they wore made them too conspicuous, for they knew what could happen if they were unlucky enough to surprise a German sentry in the wrong place; searchlights and machine-guns would suddenly sweep the entire valley and alert a swarm of armoured cars and tanks. Above all, though, they could not forget that their night's work might easily provoke the most brutal reprisals against the people of the valley.

They were not saboteurs for nothing however, and despite the privations they had endured, they were basically resilient. The nausea was quickly over and they turned to the task that lay ahead, but were unable to force either the door of the cellar or another such entry on the floor above. The darkness quite suddenly deprived Rønneberg of the support of Stronsheim and Idland but the leader, together with Kayser, found the site of the cable intake to the heavy-water installation and decided that if they were to get in at all this was the place. The mouth of the narrow tunnel was choked with snow but they kicked it away and entered a spider's web of pipes and insulated lines. Rønneberg whispered a caution to his companion and the two men wriggled through with remarkable speed and quietness considering the amount of equipment and gear they were carrying. When they came out they slipped into a room and through a door which led directly into the high-concentration plant.

The night watchman did not hear them until it was too late. Kayser poked his revolver into a generous stomach and backed him against the wall. He was an elderly man and too frightened to give any trouble. Kayser told him to take a good look at the sergeant's stripes he wore, so that he could tell his new bosses what a British uniform looked like.

Rønneberg, in the meantime, was busy laying the charges and although it had been planned to time the fuses at two minutes—which was strictly according to the British book— he decided to cut them back to thirty seconds. He was half-way through the job, and wondering if he could finish it single-handed, when the window above him was kicked in and the head and shoulders of Stronsheim appeared within its jagged frame. He had crashed the demolition party with rare determination. Rønneberg helped his comrade down but cut his fingers badly despite the rubber gloves he was wearing.

As they had been trained to do in Britain, the two men worked together easily and expertly. Stronsheim twice checked the charges, while Rønneberg completed the coupling of the fuses.

"Be careful," said the night watchman fearfully, "or you'll blow up the whole place."

"That's exactly what we intend to do," replied Kayser grimly, gently poking him in the ribs with his gun. "You'll have about twenty seconds to get out of here when we give the word."

"What about my glasses?" wailed the old man. "I'm lost without them. It will be impossible to get another pair in wartime."

"They are on the end of your nose," replied Kayser.

He looked across to the men working in the opposite corner of the cellar. Rønneberg smiled, lit both fuses and nodded his head.

"Now run like hell!" said Kayser to the watchman and gave him a push.

Outside, the covering party waited, for the longest twenty-five minutes of their lives. They had seen their comrades, dwarfed by the seven-storeyed building, melt into the embracing darkness. After that, there was nothing to be heard other than the sinister hum of machinery, and the soft-spoken and somewhat blasphemous exchanges between Poulsson and Haukelid.

They were alone together, twenty yards from the German guard hut. Poulsson carried a tommy-gun and Haukelid six hand grenades.

"If you have to heave them, don't forget to cry 'Heil Hitler' as they drop through the window," whispered Poulsson.

Elsewhere, the other men of the covering party were strung out at various points that seemed to isolate them completely from each other. There had been a lot of argument in deciding how the demolition squad should be made up, but it had all been settled amicably. It took a lot of nerve to have to wait—they all knew that. They had waited in the shadows at other times and then, as now, time seemed to come to a stop.

Storhaug, alias "The Chicken", had actually trailed Rønneberg and the others as far as he dared without violating the agreed plan and stood closer to the explosion point than the rest of the covering party. Helberg, he knew, waited near to the railway gate to get them all away quickly when the time came, but Kjelstrup had hidden himself well and could not be seen.

Calm and watchful, Storhaug could hear the sentries on the bridge talking and laughing together. It was really good to hear them because it told him that nobody so far had tumbled to the raid. His hands fondled a grenade that would help to wipe the smiles off the faces of the guards should the alarm be raised.

Suddenly, the stillness was disturbed by a slight whoosh that rose a bare note above the noise of the factory's machinery. It left Storhaug puzzled and the very mildness of it surprised Rønneberg and his comrades. They had got out by the cellar door and had not gone more than a few steps when the climax of their night's work announced itself.

Haukelid heard it with amazement. It seemed so astonishingly feeble that he thought how ridiculous it was for them to have come a thousand miles to ignite such a squib! Both he and Poulsson were caught off balance by doubt and bewilderment and, consequently, they never sighted the withdrawal of their comrades.

They decided not to move until the situation became clearer and at that moment the door of the guard hut was thrown open by a Nazi officer. Poulsson's machine-gun followed him as if operated on a swivel.

The German ambled over, his hands in the pockets of his great-coat. He rattled the main gate of the factory and found it secure. Through red-rimmed eyes Haukelid and Poulsson watched every step he made and then saw him turn at last, apparently satisfied, and stroll back to the shelter of the hut.

The men in the shadows remained silent, wondering what was to come next. In a few seconds they heard the creak of the door again as the German reappeared.

"The bastard's back," whispered Poulsson, "he must smell trouble."

The beam of a powerful torch held by the officer began to weave and pierce the shadows and Haukelid, armed with half a dozen grenades, slipped his hands in his pockets in readiness. "Could be fatal for the stupid sonofabitch," he said. He had once seen the lights of Broadway.

The beam came dangerously close and Poulsson asked, "Shall I let him have it?"

"Not yet, hold it," replied Haukelid. "I don't think he suspects anything."

Haukelid was dead right. The torch moved away from them, wavered and was then turned off. Perhaps the German believed that the noise he had heard—the incredibly gentle whoosh—was nothing more serious than the exploding of a land-mine by the sudden movement of snow in the neighbourhood. He stood for a moment, as if trying to convince himself that all was well, and then hurried back to the hut.

The watchers waited a few minutes longer, half-frozen but wary. They could not be certain that Rønneberg and his companions had succeeded—even in a small way. The noise they had heard hadn't the ring of success, but there was a way of finding out.

F

"Let's git to them thar hills," Haukelid said with more humour than he felt. Both men moved cautiously along, but not cautiously enough. Approaching the gates, they were spotted by Kjelstrup. Like some of the others, who had occupied a post on their own, he was tensed-up and in a voice that was not prepared to allow any margin for error, he twice called out quickly "Piccadilly Circus?" Haukelid and Poulsson, feeling that the evening had already provided enough excitement without the luxury of having to run into an ambush, prepared by their comrades, dropped the answering password in favour of a good, round Norwegian oath.

"What the hell's the use of a password if you don't use it?" enquired Kjelstrup acidly.

"Push off, Arne. With the trembles you've got, you'd need a haystack for a target," replied Poulsson who suddenly knew, as did Haukelid, that what they had come to do had been done. The tension was ebbing away and, despite his dourness, Kjelstrup was a happy man. The vital target *had* been destroyed and they had all got out so far, he assured them.

"Helberg," he added, "is down at the river scouting for a place to cross."

He was wrong there. Claus Helberg, Rjukan born and bred, had found time to ensure that his folk would not suffer in Gestapo reprisals. He had a brother in the Merchant Navy and his parents and three younger brothers were not far away.

He had looked after his British machine-gun with great pride many months and now he dropped the weapon, very carefully, in the snow, for the Germans to find. Then he led the way down to the Maan banks.

The river had risen because of a slight thaw and there was too much treacherous surface water over the ice. By the light of the stars they picked a likely crossing, for there was no time to waste.

As the rearguard floundered across, guns and revolvers above their heads, the air-raid sirens wailed round the valley. It was the signal for all military personnel in the area to turn out.

They looked back. Torches were flashing along the railway line, coming closer every minute. Up the road ahead, the road they must cross to gain the hills, raced enemy patrol cars.

"Nice of the bastards to keep their lights on. We can at least see where we are going," said one of them with what he thought was heavy sarcasm.

They were facing the same tortuous journey they had made hours before—a lifetime it seemed. True, the journey was in reverse, but the problems were neither greater nor smaller. Cold, the clinging discomfort of soaked clothes, and exhaustion —physical and mental. Heaving themselves up the precipitous face on the other side and each man wondering if he was climbing fast enough or holding back the others. There would be a spurt from one and then another until everybody had had a go.

They had made it, though, and sprawled for a moment's respite at the top until Helberg, as he had done at the crossing below, was ready to wave them across the road—one at a time. The last two of the nine men waiting to be signalled took a dive into a ditch when a German car, with dimmed lights, suddenly snaked round a bend. But all was well.

They did not require this incident to remind them that the road back to the Hardanger Vidda could be negotiated only by care and cunning.

Never more than two men on the same spot, in that few square feet, which might be raked by the arc of fire from a hidden machine-gun, or caught up in the blast of a heavy mortar shell, or even by the unlikely bomb from the air.

Helberg picked up his skis from the dump, slapped off the snow, ran a caressing hand down, and looked around. He remembered the tree, smitten by the forked lightning the night of the big storm, when he was but a boy. If he had a hundred kroner for every time he had glided past it, knowing he was two miles from a hot meal, he would be a rich man.

His eyes turned towards the home he could not see. What was happening down there, in his father's house, and in the houses of their neighbours now that the Nazis were aroused? Who could say or guess? So far as they knew the names of the men from the mountains were not known to the Gestapo. He looked at Poulsson as they struggled into their rucksacks.

Poulsson too was thinking of the valley. Food. Lots of food.

A drink or two. Cigarettes, then a nice cigar with coffee. And a wonderful sleep for a day and a night in a real bed which did not freeze up under you.

They sorted out the pitiful small belongings which might help to keep them alive, and struggled upwards, away from the civilisation they knew and towards the Hardanger Vidda, without a backward glance.

Helberg scouted ahead again. He had suggested to the two leaders—his old friend, Poulsson, and Rønneberg—much earlier, that the best route was a turning past a sand-pit, just before the downhill station of the cable railway, then a short trudge through the woods to the Ryes road, a narrow path running up into the mountains, built to take materials to the building of the funicular railway.

"It will," he urged, "be well-trodden and the Wehrmacht won't know one ski track from any other hole in the ground."

The idea had been agreed and later roundly cursed. The ascent to the uplands took three exhausting, shivering hours. Rucksacks dragged them backwards; skis had little bite into the wet snow and they often fell. They swore, each to his fashion, and struggled painfully up and onwards. Speed, they knew, meant security.

Poulsson and Helberg nodded thankfully to each other as they passed the level of the topmost cable-railway station. It was the end of the line for sightseers and the beginning of more trouble for the saboteurs.

The going, over virgin snow, became rougher and tougher. Their speed of advance was cut by half, and the wind was rising, whining through the doubtful protection of the pines and firs they were about to leave.

At the first ridge, leading to the Hardanger Vidda, they were hit in the face by a full westerly gale. Experienced as they were to punishment from the weather, this was as bad as they had met for many a long day. But there were nine of them and they could help each other.

They had to keep their hands over their mouths to draw breath and their faces were bleeding from the grit-laden snow which lashed them.

"The Germans will never dare to send search parties into

the mountains in this weather," said Helberg, but it seemed poor comfort at the time.

The others doubted the wisdom of his plan to break away to visit a private dump of his own.

Helberg smiled and would not argue.

"I'll see you all at Svensbu later," was all he said as he turned away and in a second was lost to sight in the swirling darkness.

Late that day, with the gale still at its fiercest, the remaining saboteurs finally reached the hut at Langsjöen. It had seemed impossible that they would ever see the refuge again, but they had battled on and suddenly one of them was opening its door. They tumbled in, threw off their rucksacks and then got down on the floor and slept as the wind howled outside.

CHAPTER 8

Most Secret—to Churchill

WINSTON CHURCHILL, man of many moods, looked his most tantalisingly cherubic that autumn evening of September, 1943.

The Prime Minister glanced at each anxious face around the big table of the War Cabinet, below the Admiralty buildings, then back to the pink "Most Secret" message that had just been handed to him.

He cleared his throat and announced:

"High concentration installation at Vemork completely destroyed on 27th-28th September. Stop. 'Gunnerside' party has gone to Sweden. Stop. Greetings."

For a moment nobody spoke. Silence was imposed by the shock of relief and those present looked at each other through the drifting haze of cigar smoke without exchanging a word.

Top-ranking Service chiefs and Ministers knew that the decoded message (tapped out by Knut Haugland on the faraway Hardanger Vidda), had lifted the threat of Nazi atomic bombing from Britain. A reprieve had been granted to two out of every five men, women and children and to one in ten, on the fringes, saved from radiation sickness worse, perhaps, than death.

In London the Cabinet had heard the great news in a message that was barren of the extraordinary drama that had been played out amid the snows of Norway. The whoosh of the explosion, funnelled by the gorge, had echoed down the valley and the dwellers there knew that a blow had been struck against the Nazis. Arbo Høeg, civil engineer in the chemical division of the Norsk Hydro, read the signs even more clearly. He was at home at the time and hoped that the saboteurs had got clear. Høeg had no intention of being seen out of doors—it was too dangerous—but he watched from behind the curtains of his bedroom window and saw the Germans arresting men, women and children who had been foolish enough to venture outside. Some time later there was a knock at the door. He had expected it, but was able to convince his interrogators that he was in bed at the time of the explosion.

Five days after the enemy search squad stomped from Høeg's white-painted timber house in Rjukan, President Roosevelt received a confidential message from Churchill and immediately dictated a directive to the United States Air Force chief in Britain. The long text, summarised, indicated that the Norwegians, under Special Operations Executive, had without casualties, put a stop to the production of heavy water. High-level bombing of Vemork could therefore be safely put at a low level of priority until further notice.

The saboteurs escaped unscathed, but there were, in fact, a few "casualties" of which the President could not have been aware. One of the Norwegian guards had to sweat out the war at Grini, but his companion was sent to a concentration camp in Germany and his family never saw him again. The foreman of the plant, and his assistant, were gaoled for a couple of weeks but released, together with others, caught in the Nazi drag-net on the night of the raid.

The names of the men who came down from the Hardanger Vidda were not then known to the enemy.

Helberg's tommy-gun—later stolen back by the Resistance —the deliberately discarded pliers and other equipment stamped "Made in Britain" thawed enemy ire and damped down reprisals.

Colonel-General von Falkenhorst had ruefully surveyed the damage done and reluctantly reported back to Berlin:

"A military job. And the best planned coup I have ever seen."

Some of the guards at Vemork quickly found themselves on the way to the Russian front. Their luckier, older comrades, who had not been on sentry duty, were removed, demoted, and suffered those indignities that the Nazis were so adept at devising.

So the impact of the explosion spread across the world and it was Churchill who, examining the incomplete file on the operation, wrote across its cover:

"What is being done for these brave men in the way of decorations?"

Two years later, on May 8th, 1945, the following awards were confirmed;

> Captain Einar Skinnarland, D.C.M., Captain Jens Poulsson, D.S.O., Lieutenant Knut Haugland, D.S.O., M.C., Lieutenant Arne Kjelstrup, M.M., Fenrik Claus Helberg, M.M., Lieutenant Joachim Rønneberg, D.S.O., Captain Knut Haukelid, D.S.O., M.C., Fenrik Kasper Idland, M.C., Fenrik Fredrik Kayser, M.M., Fenrik Hans Storhaug, M.M., Fenrik Birger Stronsheim, M.M., Private G. Syverstad, B.E.M. (Later, killed in action), Major Leif Tronstad, O.B.E. (Later, killed in action) and Dr. Jomar Brun, O.B.E. (Civil).

The night is still dark on the Norwegian mountains and the saboteurs, with the exception of Helberg, are asleep in the gale-battered hut. All tension has disappeared and the men sleep the sleep of exhaustion and yet of rare contentment. They have achieved the impossible. There is no look-out posted, for no search party could survive on Hardanger Vidda.

A shift in the westerly wind awoke Poulsson and he got up, slowly and stiffly, and went outside. It seemed to him that the gale was blowing itself out and the time had come to make a move for Lake Saure and the hut at Svensbu. He awoke the others and after a hurried meal they loaded up and closed the door of the hut after them.

They had covered only a few hundred yards when the blizzard attacked with increased fury and forced them back to the shelter. They brewed more coffee and wondered what was happening to Helberg.

"He'll be all right," Poulsson assured them. "I've never known a man who could get into and out of trouble so quickly."

He was to be proved right before many weeks had passed.

In the late afternoon the wind died away. There was very little daylight left, but they wanted to put distance between themselves and enemy patrols. They loaded up again and pushed onwards, buffeted and often bewildered by the wind changes. Darkness came so quickly and completely that Poulsson, who had hunted reindeer across the territory many times, lost the way.

He blundered into the wrong inlet at Lake Saure and retraced sodden steps, waving his companions back. For some hours he had been breaking snow ahead of the others. He was almost defeated but the thought of his mother and father, sisters and a brother kept him going. Dead or alive, his capture would have led back to the Rjukan and disaster for his family.

When the party finally stumbled down to the leaking, unlit hut, it was the most weary moment of Poulsson's life. Exhaustion could be stretched beyond human endurance.

They were weather-bound, again, after their troubled sleep, for yet another day. The wind outside screamed defiance around their ears. The word of their triumph had gone before them, along privileged enemy channels, but they were cut off from the outside world.

In their over-crowded hut, unshaven and sweat-soaked, they worried about young Helberg. A bath or any kind of washing was out of the question. During a lull in the persistent gale, Haukelid and Kjelstrup struggled far enough away from the hideaway to bury a reserve supply of clothing, shoes, food and ammunition.

They knew what the future held for them—the life of outlaws against great odds until their country was freed.

Haukelid was up a tree, fastening ammunition and vital stores to the top-most branches.

"Only way we can find them again for sure," he shouted downwards.

Kjelstrup had other ideas. He had rolled aside a big boulder, with a log as leverage, and tucked away some of their precious possessions.

From his perch Haukelid had a clear view. There was no sign of the faraway speck which would be the approaching Helberg.

They blamed the storm for his delayed appearance, but in the quiet of the next day, with the wind stilled and the snow settled, he was still missing.

On the third day they had to split up. Haukelid and Kjelstrup were to remain on the Hardanger Vidda and Joachim Rønneberg planned to lead Idland, Kayser, "The Chicken" and Stronsheim over the mountains to Stockholm. Poulsson had intended to make the dangerous trip to Oslo with his absent friend.

With better weather, German ski experts—and there were a few in Norway—might outflank and encircle them. Looking over their shoulders, they headed for the hut at Slettedal.

There they left—in a buried coffee tin—the all-important message telling of the success of their mission for the first telegraphist—Knut Haugland or Einar Skinnarland—to wing the word to London.

Poulsson, despite his firm belief in Helberg's mountain lore, was a worried man when they reached the headquarters hut at Lake Skryken. Others ate heartily from the reserve stocks of food hidden there, but Poulsson toyed around and wondered if he would ever share coffee and cakes in the cafe at Majorsteuen, near a certain underground station in Oslo. That had been the agreed rendezvous if they became separated.

They both possessed forged ration cards, but where could Helberg have got to? All manner of accidents could have happened to him when he left them on the night of the raid and, for all anyone could tell, his body might now be hidden in a snowdrift in their native wilderness.

They had expected casualties at Vemork and it was maddening to think that, every man having escaped unscathed,

Helberg's luck had run out without a friend being near to give him a hand. Poulsson felt robbed at the moment of victory and his anxiety was more acute than at any other time.

Fourteen days had gone by since the "Gunnerside" group had arrived to reinforce the others and help plan the great coup but now had come the parting of the ways. A few hours of waiting could lead to their capture and death. They shook hands with each other and Poulsson, greatly worried, headed southwards, alone.

Rønneberg and his men, in full British battle-dress, startling targets against the snow, began the 250 miles ski trek, under appalling weather conditions, to the Swedish border.

Haukelid and Kjelstrup changed into civilian clothing and packed the minimum to keep life going on their south-westerly slog across the Barren Mountains. Even then, they needed a toboggan and several sacks to carry weapons, food and equipment. They faced a five-day journey into Haukelid's old hunting ground in the Setesdal.

One minute there had been eight of them, now there were just two against the thousands of Germans who could be thrown into the hills.

"We felt rather nervous," confesses Kjelstrup, "and very lonely."

Poulsson had the same feeling later in his own capital, as he loitered beneath the clock near the underground station, watching German soldiers jostling his countrymen from the pavements into the street.

"Between five and six o'clock in the evening," Helberg had suggested. "In the rush hour."

No Helberg. He looked up and down the avenue for the last time. Dangerous to linger too long. He peered through the misted plate-glass window of the café. Hidden away in a corner was the missing scout, munching pastries and drinking coffee.

"Hullo, Jens."

They might have met that lunch-time.

"Have some cakes. They're ersatz and awful."

Heads close together, they discussed what had happened after the successful raid on Vemork, and their immediate plans.

They knew they were wanted back in Britain for further briefing. As well as badly wanted by the Gestapo.

"Two travelling together to Sweden doubles the risk," said Helberg. "I have a few things to attend to on the Hardanger Vidda."

"Will you never learn?" grumbled Poulsson. "The place will be swarming with Germans."

It was.

Haukelid and Kjelstrup saw them in the distance, methodically advancing in line abreast like so many robots. Holed up, they watched with amusement the harmless, haphazard bombing of the surrounding snowhills from the air. Became annoyed when the reindeer herds tossed up their antlers and stampeded in panic. They saw German patrols fire upon each other in the darkness, and a reconnaisance aircraft crash, killing the entire crew.

Two days after leaving their companions the couple, dodging the swarming enemy, threw back the door of the radio hut at Skarbu.

Haukelid put his boot to it, machine-gun at the ready, while his friend covered him at a distance with a Krag rifle.

Empty. But the lingering smell of cigarette smoke indicated somebody had been there not long before. They prowled around for clues among the radio equipment and weapons. The transmitters were cold.

They sat down and considered what they should do next. They had an elementary knowledge of Morse but the code signs might have been changed.

"We'll just wait until the fellows show up," decided Haukelid.

Within the hour Kjelstrup recognised Einar Skinnarland coming up from the nearby lake. He told them that Knut Haugland had skied to Slettedal to look for their message.

Knut joined them late that night.

"In a filthy temper," remembers the other Knut. "He had searched anxiously in the snow for two hours and found nothing."

"Well?" he demanded.

"According to plan." was the answer.

They found paper and pencil. In the transposed words of a Norwegian Christmas carol the historic message was coded up and sent to London.

"The measure of relief brought by that brief signal to Chiltern Court is difficult to imagine today," says Colonel Wilson. "The news was flashed to the War Cabinet, the Chiefs of Staff and other interested circles.

"Tronstad and Dr. Brun,[1] who had been smuggled out from Stockholm after abandoning his job at Norsk Hydro, realised how deadly was the blow struck at Nazi plans to subdue Britain. Tronstad had helped to design the installation and Brun had reluctantly supervised the day-by-day operations until he threw up everything and escaped.

"But the job on the Hardanger Vidda—that name haunts me—was far from finished," recollects Colonel Wilson. "The economic potential of Norway needed protection against the time when the Germans, facing defeat, would leave ruin and desolation behind them. Tronstad pressed this point all the time. He wanted to see for himself that all was in order. In the end it cost him his life.

"Meantime, the Milorg and Home Front movement needed guidance, instructors, arms. Haukelid, code-named 'Bonzo' had been kept in the Telemark with Kjelstrup for just this purpose. I worried about them. The audacity of the raid on Vemork must have infuriated the enemy."

Knut and Arne shared his thinking.

Haukelid, Kjelstrup, Haugland and Skinnarland spent only a night at Skarbu.

"At first light we get the hell out of here," said Haukelid, as he closed his eyes and was asleep immediately. That night his tommy-gun was within easy reach.

---

[1] His son, Helge, was born at Stockton-on-Tees during the war. Such were the security measures that the birth was registered under another surname until it was safe.

Over the breakfast of coffee, which was hot, and plates of groats, which were cold, they discussed future tactics. They would go westwards, as planned and an old abandoned shooting box would serve as a pivot point, the post-office of their wilderness for "the Scout-master" in London.

The telegraphists—Haugland and Skinnarland—rapidly improving his speed—would find any important messages there if the other couple ran into trouble.

Haukelid, above a spoonful of groats, remarked, "Old 'Tom Mix' at the Southampton training base always said that a pistol was a man's best friend. You'll find one of ours lashed to the top branches of a tree at Svensbu." He explained just where it could be recovered.

"We'll bog down at the Nilsbu hut on the Hamrefjell mountain," replied Haugland. "Pretty safe there. The Germans must be getting close to a fix on this place. Nilsbu is near enough for Einar too when needed."

"Wonder what has happened to Rønneberg and his lot?" mused Skinnarland.

"And Poulsson and Helberg," added Kjelstrup, who had lived through so many months of starvation with them.

"Do you know," he added, "that during a gale one night last year Poulsson gave a two-hour lecture on how to shoot reindeer. As if we didn't know. Then I found myself talking about plumbing for another hour. And Helberg wound up with his views on etiquette. Quite suddenly we found the night had gone. We didn't feel quite so hungry. Although we hadn't eaten, and Jens was dying for a cigarette."

Haukelid rarely smoked, but he joined the other three in their parting cigarettes.

"We'll make for the Vinje province."

He traced the route on the large-scale map—"Deutsche Heereskarte"—which had been "borrowed" from German sources by the Resistance.

The journey took two tiring days. The toboggan dragged them back and they ran into fresh snow. Late on the second night they pushed open the door of what should have been a deserted hut in the Songedal and found three startled men inside.

One of them immediately recognised Haukelid.

"We knew each other from pre-war days," Haukelid recalls. "He knew I had vanished to England about two years before. I knew he knew. We said we were on a ski-tour and they explained that they were doing some illegal hunting. We were matching each other's lies. We passed the night together, without much further conversation. The truth was that nobody wanted to know too much about the other's business."

Haukelid imagined he had slumbered well, but awakened, spine-sore and very tired. He was stiff from the long haul across the difficult territory but that did not explain the uneasy sleep. Maybe the cold bulkiness of the machine-gun, like a femur-to-ankle splint, along the damp hut wall, far enough away for anyone to grab it, had ruined his rest.

"Strange weapons for reindeers," somebody had said slyly, before the candles were snuffed out.

Kjelstrup was completely at ease. He had slept like the log he had found to latch the door, as five men shared a hut. All were dirty, soiled by the demands of the uplands. Haukelid's last bath had been in Scotland, almost three weeks before. His companion had given up dreaming about the impossible luxury of wallowing in steaming hot water months before that.

The hut stank with the smell of perspiration, laced with the acrid smell of fear. They made their mountain breakfast.

"We'll be off now," said Haukelid, when they had scoured the dishes and broomed the floor. "Going that way."

He pointed in the opposite direction to that which he intended to take, once they were out of sight. They exchanged Norwegian courtesies.

"They won't yap," he added, when out of hearing. "They'll be nice fellows."

They headed for the next hut. It happened to belong to Haukelid. Yet Kjelstrup pushed open the Langesae door while the owner, kneeling in the snow, was ready to give him covering fire.

"Welcome to your old happy hunting house," grinned his companion. "And just look at that."

Knut Haukelister, a cousin of the senior underground man, had stacked one corner of the hut with all the food he could beg, borrow or steal. And dry firewood was piled up against the cold stove.

" What a sight for sore eyes! "

It was the literal truth. Despite the snow-glasses, their eyes were red-rimmed from the strain. They were, of course, the two most important men in the Allied war effort in Scandinavia but they looked like unkempt tramps which Norwegian farm dogs would snarlingly surround, snapping and barking. And Nazi sentries would riddle without a second challenge.

Kjelstrup had a vivid red beard and Haukelid a fortnight's straggling dark growth. Beards were a big protection on the Hardanger Vidda. Shaving in the cold of that height was torture. Five minutes in the open and a kindly frost seemed to insulate the face and keep it warm.

They piled some of the small kindling and logs into the stove and touched off the fire. The sullen metallic container, so long neglected, roared with enthusiasm.

They had their lines of communication, shelter, enough food for several days, and more could be obtained in the locality. The lake and rivers teemed with trout and salmon and they had crossed a few reindeer tracks.

The word had been passed along that a man from the Vaagslid valley should casually drop past the hut every few days to see if anybody had arrived.

" I'm too well known in these parts," Haukelid told Kjelstrup. " You'd better go down to the village and tell the Milorg we are here."

Only three trusted Resistance men from the area were to know of their whereabouts. Kjelstrup skied downhill. A few days later they held their first council of war.

There was good news—and bad.

Rønneberg and his men, they learned, had safely reached Stockholm without involving any villagers on the long trek.

A skeleton organisation for the day of the rising already existed in the nearby districts and the leaders chosen.

" But the Germans are not finished with you yet," they

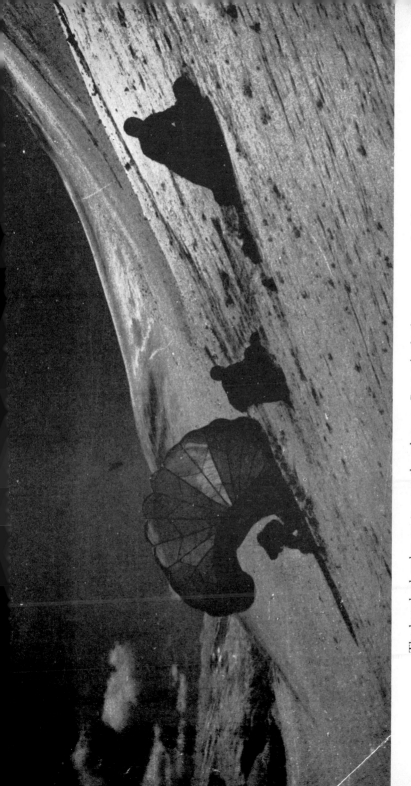

The homeland rushes up to greet the saboteurs. By a miracle there are no smashed bones on the Hardangen Vidda, the aptly named Barren Mountains.

Struggling up a radio mast in a howling gale was the least of their worries.
Starvation pulled down one shoulder. The threat of a firing squad was always
over the other.

were warned. "They have had patrols swarming on all the high ground beyond Settesdal and Telemark. Nobody helps them with information, but you had better lie low until the heat is off."

The energetic couple, back from outer space, grinned at each other. Good advice, well meant—but there was much hard slogging ahead, as discussed with Colonel Wilson and Professor Tronstad in London.

Their job was to open up cross-country routes to all regions of the Province, to brief the future leaders of the local cells. To avoid Germans, yes, although they would have been delighted to have organised a series of ambushes in spots they knew so well, and into which the enemy would have blundered to the last man. But it would have brought hundreds on their necks, with spotting aircraft overhead directing the converging hordes against two hurrying specks on the white wilderness.

"Supplies of food, whenever possible, and as little contact with the village as possible," was Haukelid's summing-up.

He peeled off several Norwegian bank-notes of high value, issued by the Bank of England, to hand to the visitors. They were, as expected, refused. There was even a suggestion, which cannot be even roughly translated, about what should be done with them!

It was exactly the response he had anticipated but, with his irreverent sense of fun, he had faithfully followed the Special Operations Executive's code for agents in overseas territories.

Hands were shaken and the three outsiders melted into the darkness.

Haukelid and Kjelstrup slept well that night, despite the feeling that they were about to buck what looked like becoming one of the worst winters of the war in Norway for those who fought the Germans from the mountains.

The baffled enemy, nervous, trigger-happy, worried by the silence of the unfamiliar surroundings, vented their fear on every hut or shooting lodge they stumbled across. These were put to the torch after the night's rest-up. Or a hand grenade, a Nazi stormtrooper's farewell, was heaved through the windows.

G

"Our sleeping bags became our homes," explains Hauke-lid. "Under peacetime summer conditions, with star-studded skies overhead, it could have been wonderful, but actually it was sheer hell. Falling snow makes a strangely warm, soft coverlet but the heat of the body melts the snow beneath and we often awakened in pools of water. We had to dry out our boots and sodden clothing in the sleeping bags too.

"Heat became a major problem. We were so high in the mountains that the nearest wood was many miles away. We dug up junipers from below the ice, a back-breaking job. Regularly we were forced to eat our meat raw. If we did not dream about nice dry stacks of wood we dreamt about well-laid tables with linen and shining cutlery, bottles of wine and huge sizzling steaks.

"At times we starved, actually starved. The supplies of food from the base hut quickly disappeared and contact with the lowlands became too dangerous for days on end. When we came to slicing our last loaves, crumbs were usually left on the plate. We drew a line with a knife through them and took turns at choosing which side of the line we wanted."

Kjelstrup, tall and broad-shouldered, suffered most. "When the war is over," he often said, "I'm going to spend my money on nothing but food. No girls. No gay times. Nothing but lots and lots of food. I'm going to become the greatest eater in Norway."

They hunted in vain.

"Even the reindeer have enough sense not to come up here," complained Haukelid bitterly, after a day in the icy mists.

The nights dragged past. It was time to contact Haugland and Skinnarland again.

Kjelstrup dropped down to Knut's cousin's house to collect fresh-baked bread for the trip. His companion followed him part of the way—and only his hunter's instinct stopped him from running into two German scouts. He sensed movement in the half light and ducked behind a small stunted birch tree, scanty enough shelter.

The Germans were breaking all the life-or-death rules of the wilds. They were too close together and talking uncon-

cernedly as their skis slapped the fresh snow. They had sub-
machine guns.

Haukelid could have reached out and touched them with
his ski-stick, or given them the unexpected end with the pistol
which had been eased from the holster. The Resistance could
have put the enemy weapons to good use.

He resisted the temptation because of what might happen
in the way of reprisals and to his friend down at the farm.

He watched them go upwards, noisily.

"Louts! " he said to himself.

Where in the hell was Arne? There would be fresh ski
marks, which even the most stupid of the enemy could track,
leading down to the little cluster of Norwegian homes.

At that moment the missing man appeared, juggling with
four loaves and slightly out of breath.

"The whole district is lousy with Huns," he said.

"I know. Two of them went by just now and really asking
for it."

They broke their fast and thought about the next move.
What was left of the bread was shared between rucksacks, a
burden but a blessing.

"A state of emergency has been declared," said Kjelstrup.
"Farmers have been warned not to leave their homes, otherwise they will be shot on sight. Seems the Germans are looking
for somebody. Us! "

"If we attempt to go over the valley to the higher part of
the Hardanger Vidda, to Haugland and Skinnarland, we shall
leave a trail that will lead them right to the radio station,"
decided Haukelid. "We'd better go back to where we came
from—and hope for more snow."

His trolls must have been active. The snows came, obliter-
ating their traces in two hours, and taking the noose from
the necks in the lowlands. They saw Germans in the distance,
but they were sticking to well-trodden paths.

The two saboteurs slithered across frozen lakes and up and
down the wind-whipped summits where there was no tell-
tale snow. Later, they were able to sleep, away from the world,
two little growing white mounds in a wilderness, and this
they did for five nights.

"Yes, we were very cold, half-frozen," says Haukelid, "but so was the trail."

On the sixth morning they shared their last scrap of food. They half succeeded in heating some water from ice by shielding the final three inches of tallow candle from the wind.

"We stank to high heaven. Any German with a sensitive nose could have found us from five miles away. Wind being in the right (or wrong) direction. We learned later that twelve thousand Nazis were scouring the territory for us."

They did not know at the time that a solitary patriot was skiing across his beloved country.

Claus Helberg had come up from Oslo again.

CHAPTER 9

Cupid on a Coach

C LAUS HELBERG, said his comrades, had the rare knack of getting into trouble quickly and out of it easily. Form, however, didn't work out too accurately when three Germans on skis charged the scout-saboteur down a hillside, only a hundred and fifty metres away.

A rangy young man with excellent reflexes, Helberg whirled round and was away in a flash. The Germans began firing at him but he had headed west, deliberately, into the sun and it made him a difficult target. Helberg glanced back occasionally at his pursuers, saw to it that he was never in a position to be cut off, and after five miles had the satisfaction of seeing two of the enemy drop far behind. They had gone as far as they were able or cared to go. Relating the facts of this encounter much later Helberg said:

"But one fellow hung on like a leech. He was in the ski championship class. I went up the Geitvassdal, drawing him away from any of the huts. It was difficult tracking at the best of times. Yet still he gained. Just a few yards every ten minutes, but too close for comfort.

"After about two hours' hard skiing and around twenty miles covered, we were both exhausted. I knew he had only a pistol, like myself. The time had come for what Knut Haukelid would have called the big show-down.

"I turned round, drew my pistol, and fired a single shot from my Colt thirty-two. I realised that the man who emptied his magazine first, at that distance, would be the loser, so I did not fire any more, but stood there as a target at fifty metres range. The German emptied his magazine at me, turned and started back.

"I sent a bullet after him. I'm not sure whether I hit him. But he began to stagger, and finally stopped, hanging over his ski-sticks. It wasn't healthy to stay around any longer, as the other two might come up at any time. I had bullets left, but I was rather tired and moved away."

Helberg knew he had been very close to death in the final stage of the chase, for although he had gambled on his opponent being too exhausted to muster a true aim, bullets from the Luger had whined over his head and one might easily have found its mark. Now, in the nervous reaction which followed his escape, Helberg's strength left him and his sense of direction, too, became impaired.

"I knew I had been nowhere near any of our huts. That was important. But this was fairly strange territory and within half an hour it was completely dark. After another two hours I tumbled over a cliff, falling forty metres. I damaged my right shoulder and fractured my right arm."

The situation had become desperate when he unscrambled himself from the snowdrift. He was alone, badly hurt and in danger of running into another patrol and this time there would be no retreat. Helberg had attempted to lose his ski tracks by taking to the ice of the Vrassjö but now he had to take a chance. Only a doctor could help him.

He switched trail, slowly and painfully, easing himself along with his left ski-stick, to Rauland, the nearest centre of civilisation. Until he reached there he had been on his feet for thirty-six hours and had covered 112 miles. At Rauland he ran into the biggest concentration of enemy top brass and anti-sabotage agents in the whole of Norway.

Quick-thinking as ever, he did not attempt to pull back when he sighted the two files of ski-troops, in silhouette, converging upon him from higher ground.

To the first Norwegian-speaking German he introduced himself. A simple local man—with a perfectly forged London identity card—who had unhappily fractured his arm and suffered painful injuries in the hunt for the saboteurs of Vemork.

The sympathetic enemy sergeant not only believed him, but sharply reprimanded for their slowness the two soldiers he had detailed to take Helberg to the nearest Army medical officer.

As they skied down to the town, Helberg began to think of the questions he would be asked and how to answer them convincingly. He wondered about the revolver he was carrying and remembered Colonel Wilson telling him that the department didn't look for heroics from their agents—the big thing was to stay alive and free. He remembered, too, the wisdom of Sherlock Holmes—that things were more safely hidden by leaving them in the open.

While the Nazi doctor bandaged him, and made him a sling, Helberg's holster and ammunition hung from a hook on the door of the surgery without attracting the attention of anyone. Helberg heard arrangements being made for him for an ambulance to take him to the Bardkeli Tourist Hotel and he had no intention of trying to sneak away.

He walked out, shuffling, the all-important weapon snatched back and hidden under his smock, and promptly bumped into two Nazi officers.

"Sorry," he apologised, giving way in the corridor. "I beg your pardon." He realised he had spoken in English and shuddered but the Germans, intent upon their own affairs, never heard him.

It seemed colder than ever. The ache of his injuries had been frozen by local injections. Yet he brushed the perspiration from his brow as he covered the last few feet to the back door of the ambulance.

He bowed his thanks to the driver and smiled at the other who sat inside with him.

"Sprechen Sie Deutsch?"

Shake of the head. That was to be expected. The soldier seemed content. But how in the hell was he to get out of this situation. There were times, he told himself, when it was wiser to drift along with events, simply because luck did not always run out quickly. If you believed in your own luck it was often enough—it got you through.

Within a matter of minutes after reaching the hotel it

seemed his good fortune had gone sour on him. He was assigned a room, a nice clean Norwegian room, with a comfortable bed. The German half-saluted and left and he had just decided on the top of the wardrobe as the hiding place for his pistol when the small hotel became alive with shouted orders and stamping feet.

Helberg found himself sandwiched in between bedrooms occupied by Reichskimmer Josef Terboven and Wilhelm Rediess, the chief of the S.S. and all German police in Norway, who had arrived, without notice, accompanied by their staffs.

Helberg had no intention of hiding in his room and went boldly down to the dining-room and ordered a meal. The Nazi chiefs occupied two large tables near the fire and he heard them discussing the search for the Norsk Hydro saboteurs. He ate slowly, as was his habit, and thought the time had come to apply himself to working out an escape route. The Bardkeli, he guessed, would be under guard and it would not be easy to get out unchallenged. Over a glass of beer he looked across at Terboven and the others and could not resist thinking to himself—if only they knew.

Just then there was a most welcome diversion. The Germans had requisitioned the finest rooms in the hotel, but they could not take over some of the high-spirited Norwegian girls. Two of them were ordered to dine with Terboven by one of his aides. They refused at first, and then were very rude throughout the entire meal.

When Terboven and party tossed their napkins down, the girls ridiculed an invitation to go up to the bedrooms with them. The situation became dark with anger, and Helberg and all those who were present guessed that there would be trouble and so it turned out.

The saboteur returned to his room and had had only an hour's uneasy sleep when he was aroused and told to get downstairs. It was almost midnight and he joined seventeen of his compatriots, among them the two girls who had defied Terboven, in the foyer of the hotel. They were taken outside and bundled into a motor coach in charge of an armed guard.

Grini concentration camp was their destination and Helberg knew that once there it would be the end of the line for him.

Despite his sling and bandages, he was roughly handled and when he tried to take a seat near the exit the guard shoved him to the back of the coach. He crouched down between the two rear seats and began to rub his arm which was painful. Luckily, he had not been searched and his pistol was secure in his shoulder holster. It was, in the circumstances, but poor consolation.

The coach was blacked out and Helberg had no opportunity of calculating just how bleak were his chances. He was, in fact, in no shape to try his luck and he was less angry with the enemy than with himself for the mishap he had suffered and realised that his injuries might, quite literally, be the death of him. Like many another man with a problem on his mind he began to whistle, until he received a hard stare from the surly guard and realised if he had to draw attention to himself it could be done to better purpose.

In a nearby seat was one of the girls who had been at the Terboven table and, quite deliberately, he began a flirtation with her that was noisy and jocular. She was a pretty girl with fine, intelligent eyes and she guessed that he had something to say that was not for the ears of the guard. They laughed and joked together and Helberg managed to whisper that there were good reasons why he should not be on the coach when it reached Grini. The girl nodded and the play continued. Helberg had seen four motor-cyclists waiting outside the hotel. They were armed with pistols and grenades and he knew that throughout the journey two of them would ride ahead and the other pair would be at the rear of the coach. Time was beginning to run out and Helberg knew that somehow or other he had to get to the front of the coach. He turned back to the girl and said, almost imperiously, "Kiss me."

Without hesitation the girl leaned forward and kissed him on the cheek—clean shaven for the first time for several months. The guard called out angrily, "Stop that nonsense or I'll teach you both a lesson."

He began to move towards them but not close enough for Helberg's liking.

" I don't know your name even, or where you come from," said the saboteur's companion.

" The less you know the better. I'm sorry about this but you won't come to any harm."

He turned and kissed her again and down the aisle lumbered the Nazi. He pushed past Helberg, turned and kicked him in the seat of his ski pants.

" Perhaps that will discourage you," he said with some satisfaction.

Helberg stage-managed the rest and got to the desired position at the exit. The guard remained where he was and turned his attention to the girl.

It was still very dark outside, but the roadside cover was very scanty. Helberg studied the driver's face and saw that the man was hardly aware of his presence. He had his eyes on the road that showed faintly from the dimmed headlights and he was not concerned with the passengers or their troubles.

The guard was still at the rear of the coach talking to the girl and, boldly, she kept the conversation going. Helberg realised that if he got away it would be because of her help. The real problem was how quickly the outriders would react when he jumped. Helberg barged the door with his uninjured shoulder and was lucky enough to nose-dive into a ditch. He scrambled up knowing that he was on the wrong side of the road to make for the hills. He heard shouts and the screech of brakes and then saw the flashes of several torches. He zig-zagged between the lights and got back on the road. Two of them were waiting for him behind the coach and there was nothing for it but to sprint in front of the coach and the headlights the driver had turned on. The saboteur's luck held and he got through but felt a thump on the back. He wondered if he had been hit by a grenade thrown by a guard too excited to pull the pin!

Running at the crouch, taking advantage of every scrap of cover, worming his way full length at times across the exposed places, Helberg gained the shelter of the deep timber.

He panted against a tree and watched the torches weave their pattern over the snow. He grinned at what must have been the shortest courtship ever. The grin vanished when he thought about the girl. She would not be victimised. Even that lout of a guard must realise she was innocent, after a few questions. There had been no proper interrogation. No names had been taken. Probably the escorts would be glad to forget they had lost one of their prisoners.

The roar of motor-cycle engines, reawakened, seemed to echo his hopes. He watched the coach pull away, through a camouflage spider's web of twigs. Poor devils, he thought. How many would land up at a *Vernichtungslager*—a camp for the doomed.

Helberg was too experienced to move, immediately. He stood stockstill, listening to the familiar welcoming sounds of his woods, completely relaxed, but alert to the first alien noise.

He had no food, no skis, but he patted below his armpit. He had that. Convinced, after about an hour, that the enemy had not left men behind in ambush, he headed towards a farm-house he knew of old. He needed skis and food.

He knew that he did not dare venture on to the snow-ploughed roads. Once a prisoner was enough. There might be a blast of fire around any bend. The going was demanding and he was exhausted when he tapped on the window. His shoulder ached, worse than ever.

Came the sudden change. The transition from the chilly and threatening outer darkness to the warmth of a Norwegian welcome. Heat, light, food were his for the asking. Skis, well-waxed, were brought down from the loft. He was pressed to stay the night but knew the punishment for harbouring the likes of him—and he needed a doctor badly.

The farmer traced out a rough route on a sheet of paper, circling loyalist homes, marking a cross on doubtful places.

"I landed up in a padded cell in a lunatic asylum," says Helberg. "Unkind friends have since suggested that it was not before time."

In his happy-go-lucky but determined way he travelled many lonely miles before he reached the hospital. In those days decent Norwegian doctors never asked too many questions. A man with bullet wounds could be left on the doorstep, after the hurrying footsteps came to the pulled alarm bell.

Helberg was lucky at the hospital. He was not entirely unknown. The doctor fixed up his shoulder again and then had him led away to the insane block. "Dangerous lunatic" was scrawled across his case history. Until the arm healed he knew no German would disturb him. He was right. He saw enemy soldiers in the distance through the small barred window but nobody bothered him. Helberg just lay back on his cot and rested up, thinking what a crazy world it was indeed.

Hatred came back to him when he heard the wails and whimpering from the woman along the corridor who had been raped into insanity by the Germans.

Quite soon Helberg began to make plans to cross the border into Sweden. From there he would be able to return to Britain. He knew a good contact man at the British Legation —Malcolm Munthe, a relative of the author-philosopher.

The fracture healed quicker than most of the kind and it was then Resistance headquarters in Sweden asked Knut Haugland in the mountains to meet a man at Baerum near the Lier ridge and give him every assistance to reach the Swedish frontier.

At the appointed place, to the minute, Haugland shook hands with Helberg again.

A few hours later one turned back to the Hardanger Vidda. The other headed east, on the first lap of the long trip to Stockholm.

CHAPTER 10

Brief Reunion

O N the sixth night after the raiding party had separated
and gone their different ways, Haukelid and Kjelstrup,
harried and hungry, made the long, tortuous trek in
the half-light and darkness to Suldal. There they had holed
up in a cave hidden in a wood and had been able to get their
clothes partly dry. As usual, they were without food and
decided to make for a farm at Nordmork. It was a dangerous
decision because the whole area was swarming with enemy
patrols and, indeed, there was a distinct chance of finding a
reception committee awaiting them at their destination. But
they were in luck and at Nordmork the farmer there gave
them, and generously, herring from his barrel and bread and
potatoes.

It was a wonderful treat for the starved men and they
went back into hiding again to await news from the
farmer that the Germans had called off the search for the
saboteurs who had wrecked the heavy-water plant. During
this time the two men worried over the possibility of their
tracks to the farm being discovered and hence a repetition
of what had become known as the Televaag tragedy—one
of the most serious blows ever delivered against Norwegian
resistance.

On the night of April 30th, 1942, Oslo radio reported that,
four days previously, two officers of the S.S. security police had
been killed while carrying out duties on an island off the
West coast. The culprits, according to Oslo, were Norwegian
nationals who had been trained in Britain and then returned

to their own country, armed and provided with explosives, for carrying out extensive acts of sabotage without regard to the interests of their fellow countrymen.

The broadcast then announced that because of their nationality eighteen Norwegians had that day been shot. The victims, whose names were read out, had been caught in the act of trying to sail to England in a fishing smack. The men, it was said, were fully armed, even to machine-guns.

Further details of the executions were given by Stavanger radio the following morning, but in the meantime the *de jure* Norwegian Government in London, though the B.B.C.'s foreign network, claimed that the victims were not caught attempting to escape, but had, in fact, been arrested some time before on grounds no stronger than suspicion. They had been subject to constant interrogation by the Gestapo and their execution was a reprisal for the shooting of the two Germans.

Both Haukelid and Kjelstrup knew the whole story which began when the British landed a saboteur at Neswick with equipment for blowing up German aircraft grounded in the Stavanger area. He was accompanied by another agent (code name "Anchor") who had a different assignment in eastern Norway. The two men spent the night at a farmhouse in Tele-vaag, but early the following morning the place was raided by the Germans who had arrived by boat from Hjellestad and gone direct to the farm. Two Gestapo officers rushed the stairs to the loft, where the two agents were hidden, and a gun battle took place that lasted several hours.

One of the saboteurs was killed and his companion badly wounded. Of the two Gestapo officers who died in the flurry of bullets, one was none other than the notorious S.S. Hauptführer Berenz, chief of counter-espionage at Bergen.

When the fight in the farmhouse came to an end, the Germans searched the place and discovered supplies of arms, ammunition, radio equipment and money. They removed the wounded saboteur (he recovered and after months of torture was finally executed) and reprisals were begun against the people of Televaag. The farmhouse and buildings were destroyed, together with seventy other houses, barns and boat-houses in the neighbourhood.

As they recalled this episode that had led to the death of eighteen of their compatriots, the two friends saw in it but another instance of a dilemma that faced men of the Resistance everywhere. Whenever they suffered a defeat, the Nazis could always be relied upon to strike back at the innocent—it was a prime tactic used in every occupied country.

Haukelid and Kjelstrup waited a week before setting off for a field hut to see if a message had been left there for them, as had been arranged. The Nazis had been there. The broken door swung on smashed hinges, but inside was a note which read: "The swine have now gone and you can come down to the farm."

Whoever had left it must have been on the enemy's heels. They had hidden fresh supplies of food on which the two men feasted until they could eat no more. After about two hours they began a second meal and wolfed food until they were almost sick. Kjelstrup, who seemed to tuck away much more than his friend, just fell asleep in his sleeping bag, a pleased smirk on his face.

The food slowly pulsed through the undernourished bodies, restoring the warmth they needed. They did not dare light the stove. A tremble of smoke in the distance might have recalled German patrols.

They rested up until midnight then tackled the fifty-mile run to Hamrefjell, in the hope that Haugland and Skinnarland had also evaded the German drag-net and had news for them.

The food had worked wonders. The mile-eating stride came back, until they lost their way in the Skundal. And Colonel Wilson almost lost one of his most determined agents.

In steep descent, Kjelstrup slipped on the hard snow crust and narrowly missed carrying Haukelid away with him, as he plunged head first down a narrow gully and over a cliff. His companion expected to find a corpse when he scrambled down to the bottom thirty minutes later, and wondered how to dispose of the body.

But the durable and lucky saboteur was alive, and cursing, with no bones broken. Looking upwards they both marvelled at his escape.

Completely helpless as he fell, he had somehow been guided down the only narrow passage free of ugly jagged outcrops.

"Any cats in your family?" asked Haukelid as they searched around for his skis and sticks and found them.

"Now for my bluddy rucksack."

Like the Norsk Hydro watchman's spectacles, it was where it ought to have been—in his case—on his back, undamaged.

Memories of the re-union at the Nilsbu hut will remain with them for the rest of their lives. Both couples had worried in case the others had been captured in the cross-country swoop which had left a tide-mark of razed shooting lodges and shanties behind the enemy's ski tracks. There had been rumours of two bearded fugitives arrested in the high lands.

Haugland and Skinnarland had been luckier than the other two. They had a tent for shelter, a paraffin stove for warmth.

"We found à sheltered spot on the Hamrefjell and just stayed put as the Nazis hunted elsewhere," explained Haugland.

"We heard at first, from a local contact, that Helberg had been taken prisoner and shot while attempting to escape. Then I saw him near Lier and guided him on his way to Sweden."

"He'll be back. You couldn't keep that one from the Rjukan for long."

It was a wild and hilarious meeting, agitated perhaps by home-distilled aquavit, with creamy milk chasers, from friendly farmers downhill, who knew how their national future was being decided in the mountains over their heads.

Their man under discussion—Helberg—was at that moment climbing into the bomb bay of a British aircraft at Stockholm.

The time was April, 1943.

Because of the Germans who had swarmed across the Hardanger Vidda after the explosion at Vemork supplies of food and ammunition could no longer be dropped by the

Calling London. CLAUS HELBERG in a calm spell for once can transmit out of doors.

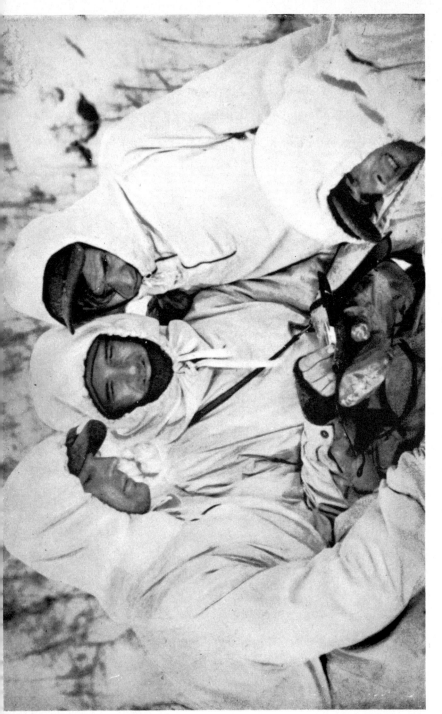

When will the others arrive? The "Grouse" group, in snow camouflage parkas, get into a

R.A.F. The four in the wilderness had to wait until the far-away autumn, when darkness came.

"Like the reindeer," said Haukelid, "we'll have to fend for ourselves."

With Skinnarland and Kjelstrup he headed northwards to the Svensbu hut. It had been half-wrecked by the enemy, but there was evidence left that Milorg units had trained there—British equipment and uniforms, boxes of rotting meat. They picked what they wanted and from there pushed on to the Skryken dump, with the exception of Kjelstrup, who returned westwards to meet Haugland again.

Mobility, movement was all important in their dangerous undercover work. In other areas Colonel Wilson's men were switching from one lonely hut to the next, instructing men for the day of the great uprising.

Between November 29th, 1942, when they parachuted into Gudbrandsdalen and the end of February, 1943, Fenrik O. Doublong and Fenrik Torbjørn Hoff (later killed in action) held eleven different courses in guerilla warfare, demolition and unarmed combat. Before they returned to Britain they had trained no less than fifty-nine potential leaders.

Comments Colonel Wilson:

"These men were all in good physical condition and of excellent morale. Yet the work done by these two agents was of much wider and lasting effect. More than anyone before they proved to Milorg the value of the training that was being given to the Linge Company across the sea. Men from the United Kingdom were no longer looked upon as dangerous interlopers, but as friends and allies who were recognised as well-trained and secure. The confidence of Milorg in their would-be helpers from overseas was at last being established on a firm basis.

"The party code-named 'Chaffinch' were dropped near Dramen on 24th January. Exactly a month later their station came on the air. The leader was the late Lieutenant Tor Stenersen with Fenrik Martin Olsen, M.C., as his helper and Fenrik Oddvar Sandersen, B.E.M., as his wireless operator. Although the original intention was for this party to work mostly in Vestfold a contact was given to the Central Leader-

H

ship and this established a direct connection which was maintained practically until the end of hostilities.

"The 'Chaffinch' station dealt with a great deal of the Central Leadership traffic. Following their first tour of four months' duty, when the party were brought back through Sweden to report and receive further instructions, the Central Leadership reported—'All three men have displayed convincing technical knowledge and a striking aptitude for imparting instruction. Their conduct and care as regards security have been exemplary.' The bonds of friendship were tied more firmly."

"The Central Leadership's messages through 'Chaffinch' at this time showed that intense interest was expressed in different parts of Norway in regard to the role which the Resistance and Milorg should now play," continues Colonel Wilson. "The ostensible reason for this was the Labour Mobilisation Ordinances that had lately been passed. During their enforcement by the Quisling Government arrests had been on the increase. Prisons were becoming more than ever overcrowded, and 170 prisoners in Grini had been sent to Germany to make room for others. Up to 200,000 men and women were affected by the decrees, but the effect, in terms of the quality of the extra labour expected, was not likely to be great. The Ordinances did, however, place Norwegians under stricter control, and gave an easy opportunity to the Quislings to remove from their sphere of activity those who were obviously opposed to the regime. It was in fact extensively used against the clergy and teachers.

"These developments resulted in agreement being reached in the main that Milorg should refrain from any overt action until Allied Forces outside Norway were in a position to cooperate with them. Fears were, however, expressed that some elements might embark on unauthorised enterprises which would bring reprisals without achieving anything of value.

"At this particular juncture, in fact, there seemed to be little doubt in high Allied circles as to the role which Resistance in Norway should fulfil. It was therefore tacitly decided that the steps to build solid ground upon which a Secret Army could stand should be continued, but that no attempt should be made to force the pace. In other words, a more natural and less forced growth of military organisation was required.

"As a directive from the Norwegian High Command (in London) to the Central Leadership of Milorg, issued at this time, stated: 'We must realise that events in Norway, which to us may appear of great importance, can hardly release Allied actions of any size unless these fit into the main performance. We must also realise that the successful issue of an operation is often dependent on strategic surprise, and that the circle of people entrusted with the secret beforehand should be as small as possible. The preparation for active support from inside during an invasion must be planned on the simplest possible lines. The difficulties of working in a German-occupied country make this necessary. Endeavours must be made to establish a quick and safe system to set in motion actions that have been planned, and we must try to keep these actions under control. The preparations must not go too far at an early stage, and they must be of a nature to allow them to be elastically adjusted to the operational plans, when these take a definite shape. The Foreign Office wishes to be in a position to decide which fighting and pioneer groups are to be mobilised or prepared for special actions. Preparations from this side will aim at establishing a communications service, through which the Allied High Command can reach groups in question quickly and safely. The Foreign Office (Norwegian) wish to lead this work from this side in close collaboration with our Allies to the greatest extent possible.'"

Haukelid was to play a major part in this, but meantime the little band on the Hardanger Vidda had to stay alive. The Germans had not uncovered the cache at Skryken. Tons of drifted snow had kept the Norwegian's silent secret. They did not presume on luck and took no chances. With the back-breaking labour so often associated with the heroics of war, they shifted what they could not bear away, further from the first dump, to the shelter of some boulders.

Even so, the snow toboggan was runner-deep with about 180 lbs of food, stores and equipment when they pushed off towards the Krossvatn, westwards.

On the first day of May they sat, resting, by the banks

of the Bjornesfjord, watching winter wearing away from the heights of the Nordmannslaag. Ice was cracking up there and there were widening streaks of open water at their feet.

Heartened by the approach of the Norwegian spring they pushed on to yet another hut at Vollane. Twenty-six miles in eight ski hours, tugging, hauling, wrestling the toboggan. They were outlaws in their own country, but they realised there were many like them.

It was about this time that Colonel Wilson was drafting their probable future in a minute to the War Cabinet. America's Overseas Strategetic Service had joined the Norwegian Foreign Office—Special Operations Executive link-up. What emerged was communicated to Haukelid and others in the field.

The long-term policy for Norway:

Military organisations at present in existence are designed to carry out sabotage and guerilla activities on or after D-day in the event of an Allied invasion of Norway.

Those in the more populated areas around Oslo are less likely to be prejudiced in their D-day activities by engaging in current sabotage than the organisations less favourably placed in this respect.

While continuing to seize every opportunity of attacking major sabotage targets by coup-de-main the existence of Milorg and the action on D-day must not be prejudiced. Milorg should be recommended to carry out unassisted sabotage on all possible occasions.

Whenever any open act of sabotage is committed, whether by coup-de-main or Milorg, evidence should be left on the site to indicate that the attack originated from the United Kingdom.

Targets for sabotage will be selected on the basis of the following priority:

Direct or indirect interference with coastal shipping.
Mines supplying valuable raw material to the enemy.
Fuel oil in storage or in transit.
Targets directly or indirectly connected with the maintenance and supply of U-boats.

Locomotives and rolling stock on railways, provided that damage to the German war effort is greater than harm suffered by the civil population.

Other establishments known to be contributing to the German war effort.

Colonel Wilson says: "This was a comprehensive direction, and it was obviously impossible for it to be carried out fully. For instance, attacks on railways had to be held up, although some were planned, in consequence of later S.H.A.E.F. directions. The specific points mentioned have, however, considerable interest in view of actions much later with regard to the enemy's plans for making Norway a base for operations in the Atlantic."

When he drafted his top-secret notes to a secretary for transmission to Major-General Sir Colin Gubbins, K.C.M.G., D.S.O., and M.C., Haukelid turned over uneasily in his sleeping bag below the leaking roof of the hut at Vollane.

He has confessed to a foreboding that there might be greater demands than just the relatively simple, if dangerous, job of helping to organise the Resistance forces for the Telemark territory.

At break of day he and Skinnarland moved forward again, to the next hut at Ugleflott, where Kjelstrup awaited them. Later, Skinnarland went back to Hamrefjell to rejoin Haugland and the other two ate and drank their fill. They had food for many days. Wooden boxes were ready-made stove fuel. No more broken fingernails inside their mittened hands as the stunted little juniper bushes were prized from the iced-over snow.

"We've been on our legs long enough. We'll rest a bit," they jointly decided. "There's no forty-eight hour passes up here."

The land around them was beginning to live again, slowly emerging from a barren wilderness into a place where things grew, and where hibernating animals stirred.

The first night away from the hut they wrested bunches of heather from the snow, bunch after bunch of purple peeping through the melting whiteness. The heather had made a wonderful under-blanket below the sleeping bags. The smell of summer was promised in the freshened earth. They churned their hands together and held them to their nostrils. There was no soap to spare, nor was there any running water near by. In any case they wanted to hold on to the smell, to go to sleep with it.

Both Haukelid and Kjelstrup felt that maybe the noose was slackening a little around their necks, and that the invaders might become prisoners in the not too distant future. In their isolation, they had no means of knowing what was happening in the world outside among those to whom they looked for freedom from the Nazi yoke.

As they contentedly swallowed their first ample meals for several weeks, the War Cabinet in London was sourly digesting the Intelligence analysis, with marked reference to Norway—and to heavy-water stocks.

The atomic shadow was lengthening once again across the Rjukan valley.

The directors of Norsk Hydro had failed, as they had on many occasions, in their attempts to persuade the enemy to cease production of the deuterium oxide. Since the morning after the raid, repairs had been rushed ahead and materials had been brought from every possible source in the occupied countries.

The information filtered through to London that the ominous drip-drip of doom had been speeded up. Stocks were beginning to accumulate. Something must be done.

The Combined Chiefs of Staff passed the dramatic life-and-probable-death decision on to the airfields, through the War Cabinet, after weeks of hesitation.

With the full, if grudging, consent of the Government in exile, the American Flying Fortresses of the 8th Bomber Command winged high over the Norwegian fjords. Their target? Norsk Hydro—and the heavy water.

They dodged most of the coastal flak, which withered away at the drooping end of the radio-location beams, when they dropped the showers of metal foil.

It was a heavy raid, mounted in the struggle against the intangible of the first atomic bomb ever. The magic eye crisscross sights must have been blinded by heavy cloud below.

The main objectives were the Norsk Hydro factory and the supplying power station further up the mountain. The latter was hit and three pipe lines destroyed. Only a stray bomb-splinter penetrated the installation plant, leaking away a mere 120 lbs of heavy water. One squadron, by mistake, concentrated on a fertiliser factory in the valley well below and sixteen Norwegians were killed there, while there was another victim at the bridge leading to the main Norsk Hydro buildings.

"There was great grief and bitterness over this raid," remembers Georg Nyhus, watchman again, at the plant that day.

Daylight attacks by Flying Fortresses on July 24th of the same year, on two separate targets, roused further anger in Norway. The first was on the Norsk Hydro nitrate, aluminium and magnesium works at Herøya and 167 aircraft showered 1,657 five-hundred-pound bombs. The nitrate and aluminium sections were badly damaged.

Target No. 2 was the U-boat workshops at Ladehammeren in the Trondheim naval basin. Three were gutted and three badly damaged.

Herøya was not in production at the time, and this, combined with the fact that no previous intimation of the raids had been given to any Norwegian authority, led to General Hansteen protesting to General Devers, who promised that this lack of information would not occur again.

CHAPTER 11

The Not So Barren Mountains

S PRING melts swiftly into summer in the Norwegian uplands when the sun begins to shine three-quarters of the way around the clock.

Months before the abortive American attack over Rjukan, fish swarmed in the streams and rivers of the Hardanger Vidda —the then not quite so Barren Mountains. Reindeer returned to the open places.

Knut Haukelid and Arne Kjelstrup ate substantial if monotonous meals. They moved around, gun-carrying gipsies, leaving a message in a buried tin box in one hut, suggesting a new way to build up local forces somewhere else. Among their first contacts was a determined group of youngsters at Vaagslid. In return for advice and guidance about the future which they were qualified to give, the saboteurs one day received a timely warning.

"Get out! Quickly."

German ski tracks were tracing a tapestry of danger around their known haunts and they decided to descend upon Oslo.

They tucked away their toboggan in a hide-out, and combined business with anticipated pleasure on the journey to the coast. In Ytre Vinje they met Tor Bö, who was to become a legendary regional leader in the uprising. All was well in his district, he assured them.

All was not well at Rauland, where Helberg almost met his end, for in crossing the Totokvarn the heavily-built Kjelstrup crashed through the deceptively thin ice. By the time his companion had dragged him ashore half the near-by village had turned out to help. The couple managed to evade most of the questioning and in two days, by 'bus, lifts and trains they reached Oslo.

Forewarned, they dodged and weaved around the major new control points, where ambitious Germans awaited their chance to snatch a Himmler medal presented by Hitler.

Unlike Helberg and Poulsson, they had no coffee-shop rendezvous arranged, nor had they homes to return to in their own capital city. Both places had been ransacked by the Gestapo and then taken over for billeting enemy troops. Haukelid's wife and mother had been arrested early in the war, when he had disappeared, but were released later. His father, quite unexpectedly, was allowed to go free for some time but eventually the day came when the Gestapo picked him up and he was taken to Grini. The old man had a bad time there, so much so that when he was released he was immediately admitted to hospital. He died within a few hours.

The saboteurs sought lodgings with a very old friend, Trond Five, who was active in a local net-work of growing importance. He gave them beds and went out to buy or borrow the mountain equipment that Haukelid needed.

"Keep under cover," he warned them. "This town is becoming red hot."

The men from the mountains ignored the advice from the city dweller, even though they appreciated that there was as much danger of arrest and execution at the next street corner as there was from their ski tracks on the Hardanger Vidda.

They believed Haugland was in Oslo, using his alias of Knut Strand and they wanted to contact him. Haukelid left a message with a trusted Resistance contact and two days later it was dropped through a letter box.

Young girls, many of them students, acted as couriers and messengers in the city at this time. The two fugitives, bringing bicycles, were to meet one of them on a quiet street corner.

The first girl handed them over to a second. They cycled, it seemed, along a roundabout route, probably to shake off any suspicious Germans, thought Kjelstrup.

At another street corner a third girl stood with a man. They recognised the broad shoulders right away. It was Knut

Haugland. In whispers they spoke about everything that had happened since their last farewell. The girls, standing out of hearing distance, grew impatient. After many shielded glances at their wrist watches they grew bolder and waved them beneath the noses of the talkative trio.

Then came the sleeve-jerking stage. They must break up. Haukelid and Kjelstrup had a meeting in a different part of the city. Somebody had asked to see them. It was most important.

They parted and Haukelid and Kjelstrup were guided along several streets to yet another familiar corner only to find Haugland again, with a big grin on his handsome face, and the same girl escort. Unknown to each other they had asked headquarters for meeting points. The determined girls smiled. Their job for that day was over anyway. They had guided important strangers to pin-points on the city map at the correct times and discreetly they withdrew.

"I'm not allowed to drink, and I think there may be some drinking tonight," said the seventeen-year-old sadly as she pedalled away. She was right about the drinking.

"It was a most hilarious encounter," muses Haukelid. "But through the haze of hang-overs, reunions, meetings with men scarce remembered, in the most out-of-the-way spots, we came away with a clear and most heartening picture of what was building up against the invaders of our country."

There were then more than 30,000 able-bodied men with weapons of some sort or another in Norway. Teenagers were recruiting to Milorg every week, when they felt that a sudden ending to school or University term would not be suspected by pro-Nazi neighbours. In addition there were small, extremely active forces of patriots in different localities, not linked to the central leadership in Oslo.

"The main Norwegian organisation is divided into three groups," reported Colonel Wilson to his War Cabinet superiors. "Firstly, political. Secondly, Secret Army. And thirdly, a Sabotage Group. The last-named really forms part of the Secret Army Group, and both of them take no active interest in politics.

"The Military Organisation (Milorg) is divided into a staff

with various committees and sub-sections. There is an active group in all the principal towns, and separate groups for organisation, air, Red Cross, supplies, maps, transport, propaganda, messenger service, finance, intelligence and communication between Norway and England. Milorg is constructed entirely on the cell principle and the sabotage cells take no active part whatsoever in the normal affairs of the Secret Army."

Earlier, Colonel Wilson had put on record some shrewd conclusions about the Norwegians his agents were working for, with and sometimes against.

" By the nature of their history over the past hundred years, and by outlook and characteristics, the Norwegians, in the beginning, were not well adapted to engage in underground activities. They had to learn the hard lesson of security, and learn it in the bitter school of experience. In a way, they were too naïve. Because a friend had been a friend he could never be a traitor and an informer. The number of Quislings was small, but such people did exist in almost every locality."

His strong sense of duty prevented Knut Haukelid from a last handshake and talk with his father, before the Germans took the older man to Grini and his ultimate death.

" I hid behind the door when he came seeking me," he says sadly. " Trond tactfully got rid of him. The less people who knew about my whereabouts the better it would be—for them."

They remained a full month in Oslo, shopping for those necessities that would keep them alive in the uplands. Unlike the housewives, with their curtailed lists, the prices were not so important. But they had to avoid buying related items in the same store because a pro-Nazi assistant might become suspicious.

The main items were two reliable bicycles, strong enough to stand up to rough riding in mountain country. They were hard to come by in the days of petrol rationing but a broad hint here, a casual word somewhere else, produced two heavy machines and the vital spares.

Fish hooks and nets were another problem. Half Norway seemed intent upon supplementing rations. The day of departure was viewed with mixed feelings. Even their twilight existence in the capital had been enjoyed to the full but there was work to do elsewhere.

Once away from the shadows of the tall buildings, they felt isolated again, two men dwarfed by the mountains, against the nakedness of sparsely populated areas. The wheels turned, propelled by the powerful thrust of thigh and calf muscles, developed by years of skiing. The sun was on their faces that warm 1943 summer, but there were long distances to cover.

Ytre Vinje, they had seen, was organised, the local men eager for action, but they had to set up cells for the rising in other hill districts like Suldal, Röldal and Bykle. At Röldal the cool-headed Haukelid had to back-pedal from a grave conversational danger. He had been instructed to report upon a minefield along the west frontier zone. The name on his cover identity card, which was examined at each check-point, was " Hartman ".

"And which branch of the Hartman family do you come from? " persisted two elderly women tourists. " I think we know them all, don't we dear? "

This is one you don't know, thought the agent. He had a plausible answer ready and quickly changed the subject. Then he literally bumped into a cousin of his who turned aside and pretended not to know him.

They built a hut in the mountains for the winter. Two thicknesses of stone with earth and peat between for warmth. It was named Bamsebu after a small elkhound puppy they had adopted.

It was their happiest time of the war, lazing in the sun sometimes, fishing, hunting, and, week after week, organising. Within three months the beginning of many more fighting units had been established in their territories. They travelled as tourists under the very noses of German sentries. It seemed to the two men that the enemy now sensed the upsurge of hatred, the growing national desire to fight back hard, and had become less arrogant.

Everywhere they went the plea was the same. Give us arms and ammunition. The answer, the same. The R.A.F. could do nothing until the long dark nights. Patience was what they had to preach, although they were more impatient than those they advised.

The build-up of what was to become the Home Forces spread not only in the Telemark area but across the length and width of the country. Secret communications between Norway and the outside world speeded-up. The number of listeners to the banned British Broadcasting Corporation news-cast reached the highest peak since the dread day in 1940 when the Government gave up the fight.

Illegal newspapers rolled off the presses in the most unlikely places. Flat-bed-printed in lofts, cow-sheds, garages, the operating theatre in a hospital late at night, even in a mortuary. Food was scarce—but not so scarce as the German-controlled broadcasts suggested. Spirits were as high as the hills.

They moved around, answering question and, at times, fending off politically-inspired demands from splinter groups within the Resistance. Both of them had worked hard in erecting living quarters but Haukelid had never felt fitter and stronger in his life.

Kjelstrup, on the other hand, was sick at intervals with distension of the stomach—a legacy of the winter he had spent in the frozen wilderness without proper food.

They decided he would struggle on until the black nights arrived and then make the run for Sweden. Once there he would be back in Scotland within forty-eight hours as a priority case. Haukelid would carry on the work with Skinnarland.

They knew about the broad directive laid down by General William Hansteen, Commander-in-Chief of the Norwegian Army, for the Home Front.

Norwegian units should be established in all districts where Allied forces were in action.

Support of the Allied forces would achieve its maximum value if used for liaison, intelligence, reconnaissance, and surprise attacks—by air, land and sea—against the enemy's flanks or rear.

Small detachments from Norwegian operational units must be available for the direct support of the functions of the Home Front. This involved large-scale infiltration into

Norway during the reconquest and a direct link with the Norwegian Home Front

The next stage would be the establishment of Norwegian Regional Commands in the liberated areas to assist the Allied forces in the work of administration—agricultural, industrial, military and the replacement of all forms of Nazi and Quisling rule.

Special Operations Executive's main role in all this, apart from the forays across the North Sea—Vikings in reverse—was to strengthen direct radio communications between Norway and the United Kingdom—between Sweden and Norway—within Norway for emergency use—with Norway for use in the event of an Allied invasion and for Allied, and particularly Norwegian forces in the field; to supply arms and explosives by sea and air; to train and transport Norwegian personnel into their homeland as agents, couriers, radio operators, instructors and propaganda organisers; to assist in every way possible in planning attacks against specific objectives approved by the Anglo-Norwegian Collaboration Committee, to disrupt and damage enemy activities and supplies.

It was the big briefing, at both ends. Haukelid, fit, and Kjelstrup, growing sicker in the field, were two lonely men within its framework.

Although political expediency prevented a direct radio link-up between Norway and Sweden, messages from the occupied interior were reaching London five times faster than in the earlier days.

"But we had our problems," recalls Colonel Wilson, "and I remember one particular message we received that caused a great deal of perturbation at Chiltern Court. It is amusing now, but it was a serious threat to security at the time. One of our younger men in the hills, who had been trained and left behind, was worried about his wife. His brother had smuggled up a message that she was in the last stages of pregnancy and wanted to be with her husband. It was their first baby and he was scared that in some hysterical outburst she might give something away.

"Very wisely, the regional leader gave permission for the

wife to make her way into the hills. The first we knew about this was a decoded request for a layette. I went down the corridor to the staff pool and asked one of the girls to go shopping and explained that we would supply the necessary coupons in the morning.

"The war was a couple of hours older when I checked on progress. The womenfolk were still arguing whether a blue or pink outfit should be bought!"

Three saboteurs parachuted into Norway two nights later. The containers which had been dropped before held high explosives for demolition purposes—and the layette for a new Norwegian. Blue for a boy—and so it turned out.

Haukelid and Kjelstrup also had problems which stretched across the North Sea. They learned that Oslo headquarters was sending them a young but trained radio operator called Niels Krohg, a likely lad, but there was no room at the hut for a third person and no inn where he could stay.

Haukelid called upon a local farmer, Aasmund Högetveit. They chewed grass and discussed the harvest prospects. Then came the major question. A billet—and maybe a Nazi bullet? Would Högetveit hire Krohg as a farm hand and try to forget the illicit transmitter in the loft? Nobody but the four of them would know of the dual existence. But discovery, warned Haukelid, would certainly mean a firing squad.

The farmer was a family man. He walked away for a few minutes to think things over, but he was also a patriot.

"Right," he said, when he returned—and shook hands on the strange bargain.

Haukelid had not underplayed the danger of acceptance. In addition to direction-finding units ringing the Hardanger Vidda, there were long-range stations in Germany reaching out questing aerial fingers to strangle sabotage activities at birth.

When young Niels came up from the city the increased communications doubled the risk. Skinnarland's mobile station became "Swallow Blue"—and the new, "Swallow Green"—and they transmitted from different places every other night and baffled the enemy, although there were many anxious moments.

Knut Haukelid tells of one narrow escape in his book *Skis Against the Atom* (William Kimber).

With Skinnarland he had gone to the inhabited area of Ytre Vinje to meet a contact and forward his information to London. His companion was tapping out the message when the aerial fell down and the connection was broken.

"I hurriedly climbed a fir-tree, fixed the aerial, and in a few minutes Einar was able to begin transmitting again," he says. "London was impatient. Where had we been? Einar had not been sending for long when I caught sight of a German reconnaissance plane flying low over the ridges and making straight for the hut. It began to circle over us. I warned Einar and he quickly sent a message in Q-code saying that contact would be broken off on account of enemy action and that we should resume in ten minutes if possible. I myself had fetched a rifle so as to be ready for any action in case the Germans were up to any tricks. The Storch flew on and Einar was able to begin transmitting again. Nevertheless we did not feel any too safe and took care to move that evening."

In London, Colonel Wilson heard about the incident with some uneasiness. He treated all men under his directions alike, but he reckoned his five agents in the Barren Mountains that autumn of 1943 were worth any five hundred elsewhere in Norway—not only for what they had accomplished already but for what they might yet achieve.

He brushed away forebodings as he analysed the over-all situation through the eyes of the Norwegian Section of Special Operations Executive. The change in the official attitude of Sweden, diplomatically prompted perhaps by western victories overseas, had made his war job so much easier.

The Foreign Office in Stockholm, clutching at its neutrality like an anxious virgin, had announced that from August 15th the passage of German war materials to Norway and Finland through Sweden would be banned. Five days' grace after that date would be given to men going to or returning from Germany on leave.

A strictly neutral Sweden, where the all-important ball bearings practically grew on every street corner in the industrial districts, was just as useful to Berlin as to London and

Washington. The new edict forced the German Navy into escorting all merchantmen carrying men and materials, which had been delivered previously by Swedish rail, to the northern ports and towns.

Sabotage made simpler, thought Colonel Wilson. The sea lanes between Oslo and Trondheim—where lurked the barnacle-encrusted Nazi battle fleet—were considered too dangerous. He quickly learned that the enemy intention was to transfer as much traffic as possible to Trondheim by Norwegian railways for sea passage.

He also had details which proved that the Germans intended to build up the southern ports of Fredrikstad and Larvik in moving troops to Denmark. The situation called for Chiltern Court conferences with the Danish Section, R.A.F. and American Airforce liaison officers in attendance. The sequel was a heavier weight of Allied bombs across the railway lines to Copenhagen and young Danish saboteurs, with the parachuted plastic explosives, destroying many miles of track and signal boxes, stations and water tanks, in their own country.

The Ministry of Economic Warfare in London estimated that the switch to the sea caused by Sweden's decision forced Germany to commit 50,000 extra tons of merchant shipping weekly on the Norwegian routes, plus warships.

Another credit item in Colonel Wilson's ledger was that rapidly increasing numbers of the Royal Air Force bomber crews were becoming familiar with the treacherous and everchanging air conditions over his adopted territory. More men and many more containers were making safe landings.

Some of the war-weary pilots who touched down at their Scottish bases from yet another night mission, must have wondered why the coastal flak suddenly erupted and died, without a bomb being dropped.

Leif Per Longum of Rjukan was one of the reasons. With his band of youngsters in the valley he wiped out several anti-aircraft guns and crews around the shores of his country.

"The method was extremely simple," he says. "There was a big ammunition dump beside the mountain railway. Somehow shells were kicked off the transport sledges and later recovered by us. They were smuggled away and the powder extracted. Then we refilled them with many times the proper charge and returned them secretly to stock. The Germans could never have known what hit them when they were fired. There were many things we could do to hamper and hinder the German war effort. Small in themselves, but collectively of great nuisance value, and quite often deadly."

The enemy was not slow in recognising patriotism at work and hit back hard and brutally against many families.

Colonel Wilson learned with regret of the fate of Gunnar Eilifsen, chief of the civilian police in Oslo. Details received in London revealed that he had been dragged from his home, before the eyes of his family and neighbours, and in the presence of some of his own men, taken away and executed.

He had failed, claimed Quisling puppets of the Nazis, to conscript enough labour forces. Too many able-bodied men, and women, across the country, were becoming saboteurs, instead of serfs. His death was linked with the incorporation of the Norwegian police, Quisling's swelling bodyguard and the despised Hird men into the so-called Armed Forces in Norway and with the arrest of Norwegian Army officers, who had been released before the invasion of 1940, or who were on the Reserve list.

Wilson believed that the Nazis had become fearful of the likelihood of major Allied landings and more than ever were prepared to deal ruthlessly with any sign of civil disobedience and resistance.

The occupying forces ran true to Teutonic form and stories of Norwegian girls forced to serve the invaders aroused public fury, as did of course the murder of Commandant Eilifsen, who had resisted increasing demands for the supply of "lovely Nordic beauties". The order for his death was given by Quisling as the result of pressure from his Nazi masters. The arrest of Norwegian army officers was not, in the view of the Special Operations Executive, any great handicap to the Resistance.

"The Secret Military Organisation may consider itself handicapped, but the formation and organisation of Resistance groups need not necessarily be adversely affected. There is some reason to suppose that the absence of these officers may be beneficial. They were very conservative in outlook, and not really alive to modern methods of total warfare. They were inclined to demand the high places and to keep down the younger, more energetic and more aggressive elements.

"There is apprehension that another wave of terrorism may wash over the Norwegian people, which will entail loss of life and much suffering. Such will tend to stiffen rather than weaken the feeling of Resistance.

"Emphasis must, however, be laid on the increasing importance of Norwegian refugees in Sweden. Every step possible should be taken to secure their organisation and training. They may yet prove the first to march into Norway. Their effect on political questions may be considerable."

In the mountains, Haukelid and Kjelstrup were unconcerned with questions of politics. All they thought and dreamed about was food.

CHAPTER 12

Manna—From The Clouds

THE belated, long-awaited miracle happened at last, but manna—food and weapons—came not directly from heaven, but fell through the clouds from the bomb-bays of high-flying Halifaxes. Haukelid and his friend knew little about it at first.

The former was sitting in his underpants, alone, before a glowing stove in the hut at Bamsebu when the drone of engines jerked his head erect.

He dashed outdoors, bare-footed, to listen. Each time the bomber turned away to begin another dangerous circuit he whipped back into the hut to grab another item of warm clothing.

By the time he was fully dressed the overhead noise died away, headed for Britain, in the moon-lit darkness. It was September and the moon was in the last quarter.

He sat down and cried, the puppy nuzzling his knees in sympathy.

Five overhead circles of futility. Nothing dropped. And he could vividly imagine what had been in the containers lying in the bomb-bays. No N.A.A.F.I. nonsense, but a special delivery—" We deliver anywhere "—from the locked back rooms of the West-End food stores and of course weapons and ammunition wiped with anti-freeze oil.

He loaded his squat little pipe with the last of the tobacco, but when he tamped it down the bowl was only half-filled.

Kjelstrup burst into the hut a day later without knocking, which was unwise, because seldom was a weapon of some sort more than a few inches from their hands, awake or asleep.

"Where is it?" he demanded.

He had been fifty miles away, re-arranging scheduled radio contact times through Einar Skinnarland with London.

"Where is what?"

"The drop."

"There's been no drop. There was a bomber overhead, but he went home to afternoon tea."

"London says there's been a drop in this immediate area. I heard for myself."

"Nonsense! I can't believe it. But we'll have a scout around."

They split up and quartered the hut in widening tracks.

Providence had been kind, as with the biblical ancients. A few feet either way and semi-starvation would have been their continuing lot. They found the first container on a narrow spit of land which jutted into their fish lake. The remainder had dropped into the water on each side and but for the marker all would have disappeared. The excursions into the ice-cold lake were unpleasant but rewarding.

They got the other containers ashore and up to the hut and gloated over five hundred pounds of chocolate, sweet biscuits, tinned fruit, jam, corned beef, dried fruit, coffee, tea —and the all-important tobacco, They also had a new radio receiver to keep them in touch with the outside world. And the outside world had not forgotten them.

They celebrated the Christmas of the previous year that September evening and read King Haakon's 1942 greetings to his armed forces everywhere. There was no turkey with trimmings but there was just about everything else. Haukelid puffed contentedly on his pipe when they turned to the more serious business of the weapons. Some of the ammunition had been ruined by the immersion but the guns were all in good trim.

"The fellows will be delighted with their belated Christmas present," said Haukelid grimly.

A few days later and the moment of parting had arrived for two men who had been together for so long under the worst possible conditions. They shook hands and smiled at each other. Kjelstrup was heading for Sweden with Tor Vinje, the local leader—to pass on information in Britain and receive further training.

Haukelid's sadness as he packed his rucksack and locked up the hut turned to frustration when he hit the heavy snows of Sauerflott. The men in the mountains had several hiding places below overhanging boulders and he found one of them and finally made tea over a fire of heather twigs.

In the morning he had to tunnel his way out and took four hours to cover a distance which would normally have taken a quarter of that time. With half the day gone, falling into and struggling out of snow holes, he reached Skinnarland, who had news for him. The Germans had sent another large-scale expedition over the Hardanger Vidda. "There are at least 150 men at Vaagslid," Skinnarland said.

The agents were not worried, secure in their local knowledge, only glad that their activities were tying down so many of the enemy.

In Chiltern Court, London, two other associates, attempting to master-mind the efforts among the faraway glaciers, precipices—and "hundreds of square miles of sweet damn-all" as the saboteurs had learned to say—echoed this satisfaction.

Colonel Wilson and Professor Tronstad, civilians called to the strangest kind of arms, two vastly different, but somehow integrated, personalities felt that the tide was turning in their favour.

A second successful parachute drop over Hamrefjell might have triggered off the renewed German action across the Hardanger Vidda, but more and more weapons for the rising were dropping into Norway and swiftly smuggled away into hiding for N-Day.

In Sweden, a suggestion made by Mr. Peter Tennant, British Press Attache, acting for Special Operations Executive, had received a grudging nod of approval from the Government. A so-called police school for fifty-four Norwegians had begun training schedules three months before at Gottrara.

By the time Kjelstrup passed through Stockholm he learned over a farewell drink with some old friends that a thousand of his countrymen had been passed out. It was heartening news. He boarded his aircraft light-hearted, and, as he confesses, rather light-headed.

The German ambassador, reading his newspaper, was of another mind and the Swedish Prime Minister was forced to announce through the State Information Board that "permission has been granted for a number of Norwegians to undergo police training, including limited shooting practice. This training has been in progress for some time and is under Swedish supervision."

Captain Evinge, former Commander of the Linge Company, had been flown into Stockholm for duty with the Police Battalions, as they became. He reported back that all was working out at his end. Only the background was different —the big Swedish buildings, instead of the moors of Aviemore.

On the Hardanger Vidda, as the dark nights came down, Haukelid and Skinnarland centred their personal anxiety on the likely severity of the approaching winter. They had more and better British-sent equipment and stores than ever before. Their big problem was wood for the stoves in the huts where they lived for a night or two nights at a time. That, and fresh meat to keep skiing strength in their bodies.

The daylight hours, drawing in, were fully occupied with fishing, cooking, wood-carrying and shelter-building. Skinnarland had become a first-class telegraphist, sending regular and accurate messages about the growing organisation to London and became known as the most proficient operator in southern Norway.

Haukelid was the hunter. He knew they must cache several gutted reindeer carcasses at different places in the natural refrigerator of the wilds, the deep snow banks, before winter took over completely. He left his companion hovering over his set and skied towards Sauerflott.

Both men regularly wore uniforms, for warmth and for patriotic reasons, but on the trip he had slipped into his white camouflage smock.

He found a herd by the Ormetjönn and skied, bent double, to within two hundred yards before one of the cows grunted and heaved herself upright. The range was easy but Haukelid's rifle misfired not once but several times and by then the herd, stampeding, had scattered in all directions.

He went to a hut he knew of, made a fire and warmed the mainspring of the weapon as hot as he dared. The paralysing cold had seized up the oil around the spring. The fire was a temptation. The weather outside was thirteen degrees below zero. But they needed meat.

He stalked another herd near Stæra. The rifle misfired again and when he returned to the base hut he had covered fifty miles. Before Skinnarland could jibe at his empty-handed return he threw the unloaded rifle at him with a few well-chosen words.

"Considering the circumstances under which we lived it was quite remarkable how few serious quarrels there were," mused Haukelid. "When we were all together before Vemork, practically living in each other's pockets, I never heard a sharp word or argument. Once I marched out of the hut in a temper and spent the night in my sleeping bag in the snow when Skinnarland criticised my shooting. A silly thing to do, but otherwise all was peaceful.

"Our relations with the farmers were also good. When the heavy snows came one old chap put snowshoes on his horse and dragged wood for us as far into the hills as he could penetrate. But the tragedy of Televaag was always at the back of our minds. He would have been shot without question if he had been discovered. And he did not risk his life for the little presents of tobacco and coffee we could give or information of where reindeer could be found. He did it for Norway."

Throughout early winter they lived out their days and nights in solitude. There was lessening radio traffic to or from Skinnarland's set, but they knew that other areas were very active, building up resistance for the day of the rising.

Under their odd code names another ten stations were operating to fixed schedules. "Baron Red" had been based in south Nordland. Despite the Gestapo swoop, "Lark" had been re-established at Trondheim, keeping a watchful eye on the battleship *Tirpitz* and her attendant cruisers and destroyers. "Antrum" was maintaining most satisfactory and useful communication from Aalesund. "Pheasant" was working east of Voss, but with some contact with Bergen.

"Cheese A", after silence since April, had come on the air again from Vest-Agder, and "Chaffinch" in Vestfold was being reinforced. "Thrush" had been set up in Østfold and "Anvil" was back from Gudbrandsdalen.

In Oslo "Plover" began transmitting again and Colonel Wilson sent in Knut Haugland as wireless operator. Two stations had been crossed off the "Scoutmaster's" list. "Carhampton" and "Raven" had been overrun by the Gestapo and destroyed.

Haugland, with the new shared code-name of "Curlew", dropped from the same flight as three other undercover agents, and landed feet first into trouble, almost sharing the fate of the Norwegians taken by the Germans.

He buried his parachute and dodged his way into Kongsberg, that straggling main street town of timbered houses, overlooked by the enormous church, which seats a congregation of one thousand, but is rarely filled.

Britain had given Haugland a Military Cross for the Vemork adventure and Colonel Wilson had returned him to Norway as chief wireless operator to the Central Leadership in the capital. He felt that his mission was bringing him nearer home, in more ways than one.

Yet there were lights in the house of his Kongsberg contact and friend. Too many lights, he thought. He watched from a distance, tucked into the shadows of a doorway. There was no good reason why his man should be on any suspect list and he needed help to reach Oslo.

After minutes of indecision, which brought perspiration to his forehead, despite the intense cold, he marched forward and pressed the buzzer.

The first glance at the face of the frightened woman who answered the door bell told him all he wanted to know.

He turned about and literally into the arms of the Gestapo reinforcements.

They rushed him inside. Practised hands ran over his body.

His rucksack was jerked from his shoulders and searched, while questions were barked at him from all corners of the living room.

They found the radio components—"but obviously didn't know what they were," recalls Haugland.

In answer to a telephone call from his worried underlings, the Area Gestapo Deputy Chief, Fehmer, pulled up in a car with a screaming of brakes.

"The noise sent a chill down my sweating spine," says Haugland. "Once experts examined the contents of my rucksack it would be the end of the road for me."

It was the slimmest of chances, but there was no other way out. He was thrown the rucksack to carry and bundled from the room. Two Germans went ahead and a couple breathed down his neck. All were armed.

He paused on the top step of the house, looked around quickly, then jumped sideways to land in the ice and snow of the road. As he rolled over, recovering from the impact, a bullet smacked into the rucksack.

While the enemy were rushing for their cars he was running, panting, head down, weaving, and keeping away from any lights. He raced up one intersection and down the next, then paused for breath in a dark archway. Getting out of town was the problem. He waited, although every nerve rebelled. Mentally he mapped his break-out route.

He was safely on the outskirts when the engine of a patrol car roared behind him in the near distance. There was the scantiest of cover on either side. But there was a manhole under his feet.

He pulled the cover away and dropped into the darkness, without injury.

"I was glad to reach Oslo and take over my new duties," he says simply.

The second man who dropped with Knut Haugland was an agent of many aliases, who established the Milorg Oslo–Stockholm courier route. He was known at first to those in London simply as "Number 24" but he became "Private Erling Fjeld" when he was parachuted back to Norway. After the Liberation he surfaced in his real name of Gunnar

Sønsteby[1], gleefully waving a German pass so describing him.

The third man of the four was unlucky. Lieutenant Tor Stenersen had done more than most to forge a link of confidence between the Central Leadership and London. He returned to his native land to help in consolidating the Resistance in the Vestfold district, but was surprised in his flat at Drammensveien 107, Olso, two weeks before Christmas, following the arrest of a Milorg man who knew the address.

Although Stenersen was able to cover the escape of another Milorg man and his own second-in-command, Fenrik Martin Olsen, M.C., he was unable himself to get clear, shot in the neck and head and taken to Akers Hospital. Four months later he attempted to escape but was shot in the leg and recaptured.

Gestapo interrogators beat him to death.

In the mountains Haukelid and Skinnarland knew nothing of this until much later. Came Christmas and against all orders they added " MX "—Merry Christmas—to their last message before the holiday.

"Holiday! " exclaimed Haukelid wryly. Yet the quickly returned "MXT"—Merry Christmas. Thanks—flashed by the English girl at the other end lightened their spirits.

They collected some shrub branches and built a Christmas tree inside the hut, then sat around eating a meal of reindeer meat and British chocolate. Minutes of precious battery time were spent on a seasonal programme from Portland Place.

On Boxing Day the isolation at that time of the year became unbearable. They knew that the village at Vaagslid was snowed in and that they could not be taken by surprise. They skied down in full uniform, two latter-day Santa Clauses, with gifts of chocolate, dried fruit, coffee and tobacco.

[1] " The probability was that Gunnar was the most intelligent, the most efficient, and the most productive agent in Norway," says Colonel Wilson.

There was a party which lasted well into the night, each villager contributing food and drink from their rationed stocks.

"And some of that home-made wine was pretty heady stuff," remembers Haukelid.

At first light they went back to the uplands, following winter roads and sledge tracks until they could break fresh snow without leaving a trail leading to Vaagslid. That was their constant worry when they went to the inhabited places. Often they had to make a detour of many miles to visit some lonely farm.

Inactivity after Christmas induced a feeling of restlessness and they stole a gramophone and a few records from a hut, leaving the estimated value in banknotes for the owner.

The novelty soon wore off and the repeated playing by each of them of their favourite disc infuriated them. Skinnarland smashed Haukelid's choice and found the compliment returned. It was a most happy solution.

Laughs were rare enough on the Hardanger Vidda in the early weeks of 1944. Both, in their different ways, had a foreboding that serious and dangerous work would be demanded of them at any moment, yet the time dragged. They slept in the short daylight periods and did whatever was necessary at night from hunting to maintaining their contacts. They were nocturnal, like some animals.

Six months before, the Tronstad-inspired signal from London had worried them : —

> *Most important to obtain exact information about conditions and volume of present production at Vemork and Notodden Stop When is final production expected to recommence Stop How is the product transported Stop When was production process resumed End.*

When the Norwegian scientist-turned-soldier had helped to brief the two groups who had swooped on Vemork, he had told them that blowing up the heavy-water concentration alone, without concern for the remainder of the basement plant, meant a stoppage of Nazi atomic ambitions for at least eighteen months.

That was why they had cached half their explosives at Lake Skryken, when the second parachute drop from Wick had been switched well away from the target area because of enemy activity.

The reports he had subsequently received from them must have caused some niggling doubts in the professor's mind. Their sources at Norsk Hydro had told them that the enemy had succeeded in beginning the deuterium-oxide process all over again, in a short five months. It had been done by shipping available stocks of heavy water back from Hamburg and recharging the repaired installation.

The distillation processes to produce 99.8 per cent pure heavy water from ordinary water at that time took two years. The Germans must have guessed it was unlikely that the war would last until then. The Germans needed a minimum of five tons for the first atomic bomb and part of the three-and-a-quarter tons in Germany was shipped to Vemork. It was not a question of highly dangerous coals to Newcastle. The stuff was relatively harmless by itself, just a harnessing agent to nuclear fission. But the raid by the Norwegians had blown sky high their chances of producing the first A-bomb unless they beat the clock. There was no question of beginning all over again. They had to start at the half-way mark and sacrifice therefore some of the heavy water from Hamburg to "prime" the apparatus.

Haukelid and the others had sensed growing apprehension in London when they learned about the semi-successful Flying Fortress raid over the Rjukan valley. Chiltern Court had asked:

> Please send earliest possible information regarding last American air attack in your district.

These signals among the routine radio traffic stood out like the antlers of a dead elk in the snow.

The saboteurs anticipated a bigger burden than trusses of iced-up wood, melting on their uniformed shoulders, each time they tapped out their code-sign to London. Meanwhile, the less dramatic, but all-important job of encouraging every fit man to a state of readiness for the rising, occupied the short daylight hours and kept them swooping in the moonlight towards the isolated farms and meeting places of small but expanding cells, swirling around the outcrops of back-breaking boulders.

Sometimes it was beautifully dangerous. The moon glade led them downwards, across fine, fresh unbroken snow. They felt as free as the few birds and the reindeer around. They were living, not as animals, but like animals. The response to each hurried visit was rewarding.

"Ytre Vinje was solidly behind us," says Haukelid.

They stayed at Bö farm in Bögrend.

"To enter this mountain farm-house and talk to Olav Bö was an experience," muses Haukelid in *Skis Against the Atom*.

"If we ever doubted the Norwegian people's ability and determination to hold out, we only needed to go to the farms in Vinje and Vaagslid. We felt that these people could endure generations of occupation and oppression. When a farmer with his family and his livestock and his land—which he could hardly carry with him if he moved—felt that he could take part in the struggle in any way, another man, who had only himself to look after, ought to be able to go on taking risks."

They took their risks.

Towards the end of January, 1944, Haukelid made a trip westward and returned through Rauland. He was worried by the heavy ski tracks on the way back and took to the near-by mountain ridge as a security measure.

When he dropped down to a friendly farm he was greeted with: "Thank God. You didn't run into them."

"Them?"

"The Germans have patrols, bigger than ever, combing the mountains. We had fifteen of the bastards here this morning."

The farmer knew nothing more. Just the visit, and rumours. It seemed that there was a penetrating hundred miles upwards sweep from Rjukan by the enemy. Haukelid wanted to know the reason and hurried on to the agreed rendezvous at the hut at Nilsbu. He found that

Skinnarland had a companion, Rolf Sörlie, young, tough Resistance man from the valley. His news was alarming.

On orders from Milorg in Oslo, the Rjukan men had mobilised and sought the security of the hills they knew. Two to three hundred of them, ill-equipped and insufficiently armed. Helberg's machine-gun, stolen back from the local garrison, after the leaders there had time to study its "Made in England" stamp, was about the only automatic weapon to their hands.

They had any amount of home-made grenades packed with rusting nails and broken glass splinters, one Krag rifle between two—and little food. The factories in Rjukan and Notodden were running down because of the missing workers and the Nazis were out for blood.

Skinnarland looked at Haukelid. This could trigger off the premature avalanche of vengeance they hoped to avoid until all was ready. It could lead to the futile loss of Norwegian lives up and down the country—this brave but stupid stand against German forces much superior in manpower and everything else.

"We're marked men," said Einar. "You must stop them, Rolf."

They set a good meal before him and wished him well on the thirty-five-mile ski trip back to Rjukan.

They coded up a signal, explaining the situation, for London.

"I hope like hell he's in time," said Haukelid. "Before they begin ticking off names and addresses and arresting women and kids."

Rolf Sörlie made it. Within four days by frantic skiing and devil-may-care driving, he had his neighbours back at work. There were only a few detentions, and the Milorg men were released within the week. The news was greeted with sighs of relief at the Nilsbu hut.

Then the biggest news of the war for them came over the air.

CHAPTER 13

"Norwegians Will Die"

EINAR SKINNARLAND informed London during the last days of November, 1943, that contacts at Norsk Hydro had good reason to believe the Nazis were considering shipping the entire reserve of heavy water to Germany and probably the equipment used in its manufacture.

Skinnarland was asked to make any further news of the plan top priority. As far as can be ascertained, this development had caused no little alarm and despondency both to the Director of Scientific and Industrial Research and to Sir John Anderson's Special Committee in Whitehall, for it could have meant that enemy scientists had reached a critical stage in the race to perfect the first atom bomb.

A little over two months went by before Skinnarland was able to amplify his original message and on the night of February 7th, 1944, he notified London that the heavy water, in giant containers, was due for dispatch to Hamburg, probably within the week.

"We should open our big mouths," grumbled Haukelid at the lonely outpost he shared with Skinnarland, when London radioed asking if the shipment could be prevented.

The Cabinet knew what was happening and its spokesman telephoned headquarters of Special Operations Executive to emphasise its grave concern.

"The P.M. says that the delivery must, repeat must, be stopped at all costs," he told Colonel Wilson.

Norway's Government in exile shared this view and agreed

At last! The reinforcements for the big raid. The reunion on the Hardangen Vidda.

FREDRIK KAYSER.

Now COLONEL-LIEUTENANT KNUT HAUKELID, D.S.O., M.C., a war-like man who believes in trolls, the legendary people of the Norwegian mountains.

HANS STORHAUG. They nicknamed him " The Chicken ". Said the irate gamekeeper in Scotland: —" He had a ruddy great beak and looked like a chicken! "

JOACHIM RØNNEBERG, the leader of the unit.

that whatever measures were necessary to defeat the enemy plan would have to be carried out by agents in the territory without regard to the certainty of reprisals—whether the mission succeeded or not—against the local population.

Colonel Wilson occupied a flatlet along the corridor of his office and after years of sleeping out in the open found no difficulty—after a twelve-hour day—in getting off as soon as his head touched the pillow. But this night he could not pass the barrier. He heard the traffic outside and began to think, as he had on previous occasions, of the desolation and disaster that would be visited on London if the Nazis succeeded with the bomb. Nothing the Luftwaffe had ever done to destroy the city would approach the holocaust that threatened. He knew Haukelid was returning from a trip fifty miles west of Rjukan, but he guessed the couple would read the message together.

They had. And like Colonel Wilson, it was not their most sound sleep of the year.

They discussed the situation from every angle, feeding the stove with the remaining wood fuel they were not likely to need again. Young Rolf Sörlie sat listening to the talk and was able to give them the latest information from the valley.

His contacts at Norsk Hydro were certain that total destruction of the heavy water in transit would delay the Nazi atomic bomb for two years, and surely the war by then would be over.

Engineer Larsen had contaminated the stocks with oil drippings as often as possible and had found other ways of delaying production, until discovery and a firing squad seemed inevitable. Now the Nazis planned to withdraw everything from the installation—more deuterium oxide in the earliest form than had been blown up in the affair at Vemork, and twice as much again in the secondary stage of preparation.

The enemy, warned Sörlie, were taking no chances this time. Two extra battalions of guard troops had arrived at Rjukan, for dispersal over the area, with extra Gestapo to keep an eye on everything. A direct attack on the factory was out of the question. The windows of the lower storeys had been walled in with steel-corsetted concrete and a number of armour-plated doors had been installed.

"Larsen says you can forget any idea of a frontal attack," added the youngster. "To even get into the plant you have to show a special pass to the sentries, then climb a staircase to the second floor, where there is a steel door, locked and chain-barred on the inside, with another guard checking you over through a peep-hole. At a rough count, there are ten times as many Germans around as on that early morning when your lot did the first damage.

"What's more, Larsen says the stuff will be contained in about seventy drums. You'd need half the Norwegian Army to blow up that lot, if you could get near it."

"Big help," said Haukelid wryly.

He had risen to the challenge like a salmon to one of his cunning artificial lures, dry flies made mainly from the trimmed feathers of the mountain birds, the wisp of animal wool, foil from his tobacco packets, and the hooks from Oslo.

"And there's a strong rumour that two scouting aircraft will be flown in to watch for any converging ski-tracks on Vemork," added Sörlie. "One of the fellows overheard talk about bringing up high octane."

"They're certainly taking no chances," said Skinnarland, propped up on his elbow in his bunk.

"Nor must we. That load of heavy water must not leave Norway." Haukelid repeated his last phrase more slowly. "Must not leave Norway. But, of course, it can. So long as it never reaches Germany. Sörlie, I want you back in the valley in the morning. Learn everything you can about the preparations there. When you return we'll give you the drill on demolition and what arms we'll need."

The plan was only half-formed in his mind when he dropped into a restless sleep. By the next night Sörlie had returned shrugging his shoulders. He unbuckled his skis and sighed.

The troops down below were S.S.-selected and the toughest. Two aircraft had touched down at the small emergency airstrip at Attraa, near the shores of the Tinnjö. They were up again immediately after re-fuelling, snooping and weaving across the mountains and valleys.

The Germans were camouflaging the heavy-water containers with "potash lye" labels, and the people of the valley were living on their nerves, wondering what would happen next.

Skinnarland and Haukelid, who knew all about the effect of prolonged anxiety, had part of the answer for their eager recruit.

During the night Haukelid had stirred.

"Einar. You awake?"

"I wasn't until you began bellowing."

"You're as fast as anybody in Norway on the British sets now."

A grunt in the darkness.

"You'll have to stay in the hills as the radio link-up with London."

"Not bluddy likely."

Haukelid drew a patient breath.

"If we buy it—as they say so charmingly in England— you'll have to go down and take over, but you know what old Wilson thinks. He'd want you up here, and he's the boss."

"I'll sleep on it." Another grunt signed him off from any further discussion.

By the time Sörlie had returned and busied himself with a meal, Skinnarland was reconciled to Haukelid's suggestion.

Between bites Sörlie sketched in some more details. All depressing.

There would be a trigger-happy guard every tenth sleeper along the railway track between Vemork and Rjukan and likely enough a pilot engine would run ahead to detonate any dynamite lashed to the tracks.

The train would wait overnight at a selected spot, but the enemy was taking no chances there. No surrounding cover within two hundred yards, and everything would be flood-lit and ringed by guards carrying machine-guns. As a further precaution the consignment would be split up at Rjukan. Half would continue by rail, the rest would be shifted by road to join up at the tiny sea port of Mel.

"How we could use the fellows who flew back to Britain; Helberg, Poulsson and the crowd."

"No time for that," answered Sörlie. "Larsen thinks the waggons will roll on the nineteenth."

"Ten days from now."

As Sörlie cleaned his empty plate with handfuls of snow outside, the other two, sabotage veterans, sat around the stove and talked.

No matter what was attempted, or where it was ventured, whether they succeeded or failed, other Norwegians must die; either at the decisive moment, or in the reprisals which would automatically follow.

"This is the way I see it," said Haukelid. "To begin with, we shall have to move in close to the enemy and that means a base overlooking the valley. If we stampede them, we have to see to it that they don't cut us off. There's no chance of creeping up on the target at source—we can't pull the same trick twice. From what Sörlie says we can forget about the cache of dynamite we hid between Vemork and Rjukan. We couldn't approach even within miles of it. All the same, we shall have to take a close look at the preparations the Nazis are making and we have, too, to get a message through to London. There's a question that has to be answered."

There was a long silence, each man busy with his own thoughts. Skinnarland was the first to speak and he recalled that he was dropped back home after only one practice parachute jump. "I admit I was plenty frightened. I hesitated and that's why I didn't quite hit the target area. It seems that I have been cooped ever since and it looks as if I shall have to be left behind," he said regretfully.

Young Sörlie was excited and enjoying himself. He said that he didn't accept everything the experts said about what could or could not be done." I've done enough of the donkey work to enjoy a bit of the fun." he said with a bright smile. He knew he was with two leaders famous among the Resistance in the South and he would have promptly obeyed any order they cared to make.

Haukelid looked at the problem as he thought the Nazis would do and in doing so he remembered the railway gate they had sneaked through and the track that snaked between the plant and the town of Rjukan that lay between the hills. Reluctantly, he decided that the enemy was taking all the precautions he himself would have taken.

Finally, a message was coded to Colonel Wilson suggesting that the destruction of the heavy water could not be achieved at Vemork, but by sinking the ferry which would take the seventy containers of heavy water out of the Tinnjö fjord.

While they awaited a reply, the two saboteurs instructed Sörlie in the use of small arms and demolition work. Later Haukelid and Sörlie moved down towards Rjukan. They had two companions.

Skinnarland had solicited the help of two Mösstrand farm hands to help them with their gear.

They skied off late on the night of February 12th. They had to cross the Mösvatn, Skinnarland's home territory, in pitch blackness and press onwards to Lake Langesjaa.

Sörlie scouted. He had made so many trips on moonless nights between Rjukan and Nilsbu that he led them straight to the selected hut, where they forced their way indoors.

After sleeping through the day they crept down on another hut overlooking the valley and then Haukelid sent the two helpers back to their homes. He and his young companion continued to sleep by day and drop down the half-mile to the town each night. They were taking chances for Terboven, through military liaison, had just been informed of further signals being picked up from "criminal gangsters in the mountains," and was handing out instructions at a Gestapo conference in a hotel room at the very moment that Haukelid and Sörlie had slipped into a house only a few paces away on the main street. They had gone there to be primed about the latest enemy moves and what they heard was hardly encouraging. Nevertheless, they were pleased to meet two newcomers, who had not long joined the Resistance. They were Gunnar Syverstad[1], a laboratory assistant at Vemork, and

---

[1] Killed in the same ambush as Professor Leif Tronstad. He was then Private Syverstad, B.E.M.

Larsen the engineer. Both men, at great risk, had been contaminating the heavy water after "Swallow" had passed on the following message to them:

> "It would be of great importance if the heavy water could be contaminated. Oil or cod-liver oil should be placed in the cells. The necessary quantity would be the equivalent of one glass of oil for the apparatus IC 14, or one coffee cup for a whole elecetrolytic tube. Care must be observed. On restarting in Germany the oil will have an effect not likely to cause suspicion."

Their efforts, British agents in Berlin had reported back, had been in vain. The heavy water had been purified within a matter of a few days.

There was some argument as to whether the safe passage of the seventy containers to Germany would really mean atomic bombs on Britain. They were realistic enough to know that their own country would never suffer. Big targets, apart from Oslo, were non-existent. Yet there were divided opinions at Vemork.

"London thinks this would mean the biggest and most disastrous explosion in history," Haukelid said. "But we'll check before we go into action."

He made the half-mile struggle uphill again, the climb that demanded around three hours of protesting muscles and backstraining effort, in order to send a messenger to Skinnarland with instructions to refer the question to London.

They had arranged a code. If Chiltern Court insisted upon sabotage the message would be that Hovden was sending down five kilos of fish. If the attempt was called off—ten kilos of fish.

Skinnarland tapped out the all-important signal.

> "Bonzo reports as follows: Our contacts at Rjukan think German method is inferior to Norwegian. They doubt if result of operation is worth reprisals. We ourselves cannot decide how important the operation is. Please reply this evening if possible."

Time was running out.

London answered quickly:

"Matter has been considered. It is thought very important that the heavy water shall be destroyed. Hope it can be done without too disastrous results. Send our best wishes for success in the work."

Haukelid received the "five kilos" telephone message with very mixed feelings down in Rjukan. He called a meeting to break the news. Present were Sörlie, Syverstad, Larsen and another Resistance man, Kjell Nielsen. They heard his message from Britain in silence. He studied the faces around the table.

"I know," he said. "It's tough. Sure it's tough—but London says there is no other way."

They talked tactics again. Instead of the third-rate barracks troops of the past, the enemy had drafted a much stronger and more alert guard group around the factory. Extra sentries had been posted to the explosives dump down the line.

"That brings us to the station across the road," said Nielsen, "but it will be swarming with them. How about Svelgfoss?"

Svelgfoss was a village between Tinnoset and Notodden on the way to the coast.

"We'd wipe the place off the map. Don't forget there will be any amount of ammonia drums—high concentrate—on the train," cautioned Larsen.

They discussed the movements of their sinister target from every angle.

"The ferry itself is the answer," Haukelid announced in the end.

He dressed as a workman and bought a trip in the ship. It was called the *Hydro*. Twenty minutes passed before he was over the deepest part of the fjord, off Hasleviken.

"That's where it must happen," he told the others on his return. "But how, a time-bomb of some kind is needed."

"Sörlie. Do you think you can scrounge some detonators? Nielsen, you buy a couple of alarm clocks. No, better still, get one. Syverstad, you buy another in a different shop. We'll meet again tomorrow night."

He toiled uphill again with Sörlie. No rucksack across his shoulders—but a heavy weight on his conscience. Maybe at a stumbling uncertain moment on the ice, he decided to join the Army after his country was liberated, without being aware of his decision.

"I had never a thought of this before," he confesses, "until it was all over. I went to our Military Academy and graduated in 1948. Perhaps it was the ferry incident. I was hunted, harried, worried. The Army proper had the delegation of death, clearly laid down. Very formal warfare. Divisional headquarters to the commanding officers in the field; passed to Battalion headquarters and sent down to the front line."

He knew that whatever plans he made he would kill some of his countrymen, who would die without even knowing why.

Next night the Gestapo could have made the biggest catch of the war in Norway, only a few doors from their Rjukan headquarters.

The most wanted saboteur, four of his determined helpers, a handful of the vital detonators, two powerful alarm clocks, to touch off a nightmare.

"That's all we need to rig the job," said Haukelid, looking over the bits and pieces on the table. The plastic explosives had been left hidden in the hut.

"Sörlie and I will take the gear up to the hills and experiment. London has moved the 'Chaffinch' crowd from the Vestfold to Skien. If anything slips up here . . ." he shrugged his shoulders, "they'll take over and sink the freighter which has been picked out to relay the stuff to Hamburg."

That night they checked the mechanism of the clocks and worked out the best way the detonators might be attached. They set the alarms, with weakened charges, for the time they wanted to waken. The real explosives were tucked away as far as possible from the ledge.

Hours later, Haukelid's stockinged feet hit the floor while he was still half asleep. Sörlie had grabbed a Sten-gun and was weaving it around through a window.

Attack?

They both looked sheepishly at the clamouring clock. The second joined in at that moment, and touched-off the other damped-down detonator.

"At least they work okay," grumbled Sörlie, setting down his Sten and crawling back into his sleeping bag.

These were the anxious nights and days of sleeping, waiting, thinking and wondering, the very trying time. Each had distant relatives, and close friends from childhood days, in the sleeping valley below. Men and women they must not warn. More important, men and women who had brought up children. Small girls and boys who might be whipped off shopping sledges or from skiing to school by men in grey uniforms and given sweets, or a deformity of arm or leg, before they cracked and bubbled out what little they knew or guessed.

These were the awful dangers they were wishing on this cleft in their mountains; to prevent the big bomb over other places which ran north, south, east and west from Piccadilly Circus.

Haukelid thought back. He remembered the night-club. The two junior officers had delighted in spending Government money in keeping him under cover, when he first touched down in Britain from Stockholm. They would probably be in the African desert or in Italy now. What was the Norwegian equivalent of "smithereens"? The first A-bomb would probably spew damage down as far as—he remembered his well-thumbed underground map. Putney, of course, where the old woman had lived. What was her name? She had taken in some of the fellows under training and treated them like her own. She had had a son, he remembered. His father never saw him. The Somme—and then Dunkirk. Two generations gone.

He stirred in his bunk, at his second awakening.

"It's a bluddy stupid world," announced the sleepy philosopher.

"You could be right," agreed Sörlie. "But how about some more sleep? We have lots of time."

Haukelid turned his face towards a knot-hole in the bleak board above his head and mentally rephrased his message to

Colonel Wilson. It was passed on by courier to Skinnarland and winged in code to London.

"Request permission to sink ferry in Tinnjö. No other way feasible. Greetings Bonzo."

The hours anticipating the answer were the longest of his life.

CHAPTER 14

Four Against a Ferry

THE borrowed car refused to start in the Rjukan back
street.

They sweated over and around it in the sub-zero
night, four Norwegians saboteurs at the beginning of the most
daring mission of the Scandinavian war—with no other transport available to get them to the seaport of Mel, the scene
of the proposed action.

Haukelid, normally a patient man, kicked at a tyre.

"You dumb, insolent brute," he said, furiously.

The flow of blasphemous invective must have had some
effect, for Engineer Larsen of Norsk Hydro ducked out from
under the bonnet, wrenched at the choke and went back to
swing the handle for the hundredth time. The engine reluctantly coughed alive.

They were, at last, on their way—exactly one precious hour
behind schedule.

Kjell Neilsen, the other engineer-conspirator at the Vemork
plant, had been made responsible to the Germans for the tapping of the installations. He found a series of plausible
reasons for delaying such operations until the Saturday afternoon to ensure that the shipment could not sail until the
Sunday, when they knew that fewer Norwegians would take
passage.

Neilsen had passed down the message that he had initialled
the consignment chit for the two trucks—bearing seventy
containers of heavy water—to move towards Mel, with a stop
in the flood-lit clearing above Rjukan.

Haukelid and Sörlie had crawled to the cliff edge and looked down. There had been their biggest target ever, starkly outlined by powerful overhead lighting, lighting which also silhouetted the giant shadows of many Germans carrying machine-guns at the ready.

"We'd need the whole of the Linge Company[1], or some lucky pin-pointing by the R.A.F. to destroy that lot," Haukelid had said. "The original ferry scheme must go through. Blast it! Doubly blast it! "

Sörlie had a good friend who aimed to travel on the ferry that Sunday morning. Gunnar Syverstad's elderly mother had her trip planned for the same day, weeks before.

To the first Haukelid had said in sorrow: — "He must not be warned, because he will alert others and the word will get round."

To Syverstad he had begged: "Keep her away. Any excuse. Lock her up in the cupboard if necessary, until the job is over."

With an instinct sharpened by his life in the wilds, he had sensed the mounting tension, the tightening noose. Larsen had heard that a Nazi telephone warning between Oslo and Rjukan had been intercepted by a Resistance switchboard operator who spoke German fluently. Gestapo headquarters, his informant had said, had been alerted to anticipate "the most fantastic sabotage" attempts.

The heavily-guarded train, Haukelid had learned, was due to leave for the port exactly—he looked at his wrist-watch—seven hours after their belated beginning. Arrival at Mel, eight o'clock on that sharp Sunday morning. Departure of the ferry, two hours later.

There was no question that the transfer of the trucks from the siding on to the 'tween-deck guide rails of the small ship would be rapid and " practically under a bridal arch of crossed bayonets and machine-guns " he had decided. That was not their big worry. What caused concern was the lack of information about anti-sabotage measures already mounted. How

---

[1] Of the 120-odd officers and men of the Linge Company, fifty gave their lives in helping to recapture Norway.

many sentries would there be and just where would they be placed? What about booby-traps?

He remembered he had helped rig one in the Commandant's lavatory cistern in Scotland and had suffered stoppage of pay and local leave, because it failed to work!

The main difficulty had been the Oslo inspired departure to the hills by the local Milorg men, destroying all connections with Mel, where renewed inquiries about enemy precautions, so soon afterwards, would have endangered the whole desperate project that he had written out so carefully in longhand; and sent to Stockholm for onwards transmission days before they scrounged the detonators and the wretched engine failed to burst into life.

Still, they were moving nicely along the short distance, to within three-quarters of a mile of the jetty.

There was a hard frozen surface over the snow that morning. It gave too much away. As they had gone much faster than planned, the whirling chains, like flails, had spurted up a wake of dirty whiteness on either side. Yet they had arrived at the selected lonely spot without challenge.

They were more than ready, but dreading, any challenge. They had sten-guns—made in knocked-up, knocked-about British back-yard armouries, small arms with ample ammunition and hand grenades. Four apiece for the trio who left the car and slinked down to the berthed ferry. Then, of course, there were the plastic explosives, the detonators and the alarm clocks.

Their real security was in the silent strangulation of any sentry who barred their way. Haukelid, the expert, led them towards their objective, both hands free and dangling by his side.

"I felt like a mobile munition factory," he confesses. "There was stuff looped across my shoulders and under my great-coat. Some of it was around my waist and my pockets bulged."

He had left the strictest instructions at the car. Those left behind had to wait no longer than two hours and to drive off immediately if they heard shots before that time had passed. Larsen was to make for Sweden, Olso first, then Stockholm.

He was the last of the Norsk Hydro engineers with the complete know-how about heavy water. They had shaken hands.

"Get across the frontier," he had said. "Report to our people in Stockholm. Everything will be laid on. Jomar Brun is waiting to welcome you in Britain. Good luck."

"And good luck to you."

And that we'll need, he thought, as they slipped in and out of the shadows of Mel station to the gang-way of the *Hydro*, a blur in the darkness. Pirates, who had chosen their own plank to walk.

The snapping of ice beneath their feet at the approach sounded like machine-gun fire to tensed-up nervous systems. Haukelid waved them down and stared hard at the inboard end of the gang-way. Not a single guard in sight, Norwegian or German. The circular sweep of both arms wordlessly asked for covering fire, if necessary.

He detached from Rolf Sörlie and Gunnar Syverstad, who melted back into the surrounding black welter of sheds, to stalk, slowly, like some outsized cat, towards the main deck.

No quarter-master. No armed sentry. He looked over his shoulder and waved the two youngsters aboard. He had the uneasy feeling that it was all far too easy.

When Sörlie and Syverstad closed in on him he nodded the way forward guided by the noise from the crew quarters. He stayed the other two with a backward flip of his hand as he listened at the door.

Poker. A rowdy game of poker was reaching a climax, and the voices were those of Norwegians. Almost the entire ship's crew were gathered together round a long table, playing poker. Only the engineer and stoker were working in the engine-room, so there was no question of going in.

They crept away and descended to the third-class accommodation and Haukelid found the hatch cover to the bilges. Before he could lift it they heard footsteps.

They dived for the cover of the nearest table, but the ferry night watchman was already framed in the doorway.

"He must have sensed that there were strangers aboard and left the poker game. Maybe he was winning," says Haukelid.

"My first thought was that we had lost. But thank God he was a good Norwegian.

"We told him that we were on the run from the Gestapo and must hide. He immediately accepted the explanation and showed us the hatch-cover we knew about. I hinted that we had some dangerous things to dump. He winked, and pointed below. No doubt many anti-Nazi packages had made the trip in the same space."

Haukelid and Syverstad went down, rung by rung, one-handed, into oily bilge water which crept, inch by inch, over their boots, and half-way up to their knees. The sacks dangled from their free hands. Well away from the cold and damaging water which chilled their feet.

Haukelid thought about Haugland diving into a man-hole in the main street in Kongsberg.

They could hear Sörlie chatting to the watchman above, probably missing every other answer, because he was listening out for any sounds of activity below his feet.

The night outside was still, much too still, with edges of moonlight fretting through the cloud breaks, to pin-point in illumination any escape route.

Haukelid looked at Syverstad in the half darkness, as they felt their way towards the bows. He was sweating too. They were trapped in this coffin of steel they had freely entered and any moment the approaching jack-boots of a squad, like undertakers, could trample across the gang-plank and pin down the lid.

Like most messages from the Norwegian saboteurs to Colonel Wilson, the next part of Haukelid's report was sheer understatement.

"We crept along the keel up to the bows," he reported. "I laid my charges in the bilges, hoping that the hole in the bows would lift the stern of the ferry and render it immediately unmanageable."

What he did not write was that in the clamminess, as they fumbled, numb-fingered, with the detonators and alarm-clocks, they never had more than a third of an inch margin for error, from blowing themselves and the ferry in showering fragments right across the Mel waterfront.

That was the tested space between the trip-hammers of the clocks and the detonators. And the detonators were linked to the plastic explosive.

Haukelid's report to London continued:

"I coupled the charges to two separate time-delay mechanisms, tied to the stringers on each side. These time-delays I had specially constructed out of the alarm clocks. I reckoned that the charge was big enough to sink the ferry in four or five minutes. I set the time-delay for 10-45 a.m. the same morning. This was the time which, as I discovered on a previous reconnaissance trip aboard the *Hydro*, would bring the ship to the best place for sinking."

He sank the plastic explosive, sausage-shaped, nineteen pounds of it, invented in France, and dropped by the R.A.F., under water in the bilges of his Norwegian ship.

He had reckoned that this would blow eleven square feet out of the side of the ferry. As the Tinnjö was narrow at its deepest point, the ideal explosive point, he could only afford a maximum of five minutes against the possibilty of hurried beaching.

"The job took time," he says. "Anxiety seemed to race ahead of accuracy to our finger-tips. But at last I was satisfied. I looked at Syverstad and nodded my head."

"Thank God," said Syverstad, backing away along the keel from the bows.

Sörlie, in his long drawn-out discussion with the watchman, had made it clear that they must all go back to Rjukan for further belongings and return to the ferry just before sailing time.

"That man is still the man on my conscience," confesses Haukelid. "I felt like Judas as I shook hands and thanked him. But what could we do? If we had cracked him over the head and carted him ashore, to leave him somewhere, tied up, or if we had taken him with us, his absence would have raised the alarm and the whole operation would have been wrecked. I just had to console myself with the thought that he was a good Norwegian and hope that he was also a good swimmer."

They did not linger over the farewells. Soft-footed as possible, they dodged their way back to the car. When they

Leap into danger. They came down from the Barren Mountains. The enemy thought their task impossible.

Norwegian Resistance men—some in snow camouflage suits—march and are inspected in the Rjukan valley, scene of their countrymen's greatest sabotage exploit.

The great day.
Liberation!

whistled at the waiting driver only five minutes of their two hours were left.

Sörlie headed for the mountains again, to rejoin Einar Skinnarland. Handshakes all round.

" I'll be back before long," promised Haukelid.

The car dropped him with Larsen near Kongsberg. They walked to the station. From there they booked tickets to Hokksund, and switched trains onwards to Drammen. From there, convinced that the trail was as cold as the weather outside, they booked for Oslo.

Half-way between Hokksund and Drammen the weary Haukelid looked at his wrist-watch. Fifteen minutes to eleven o'clock. Zero hour. What was happening on the Tinnjö?

. . . The mate of the *Hydro* wakened with a queasy stomach, and uneasy mind.

His sleep had been short and snatched, a matter of less than four hours after the poker session had ended in the usual Saturday–Sunday scowls of disappointment and beams of satisfaction.

Haukelid had peeped down through the hatch cover on the way ashore, fascinated by a fellow gambler, to see him draw the ace of spades—the death card—three times in rapid succession, when he needed almost any of the others left in the dealer's pack.

Waterfront idlers saw the burly figure successfully and expertly shepherd the German trucks on to the ferry, not guessing he had a minor hang-over and a major foreboding. Then the ring bolts were lashed down for stability, and the lines snaked aboard. They were under way and the quay drifted astern.

He might have gone to his cabin, unshaven, to freshen up. Back to the bridge.

Then it must have happened. Suddenly. Exactly to Haukelid's chosen minute.

The forepeak must have bulged outwards in the muffled underwater explosion and the ferry plunged by the head, the German waggons taking charge, wrestling away from their securing wires, and trundling along to dive to the bottom in the deepest part of the fjord.

L

The Captain, accustomed to the leisurely familiar trip, must have doubted his eyesight when all hell broke loose below his feet—and then drowned, half-guessing what had happened.

Fourteen Norwegians and four Germans lost their lives. The *Hydro* hit the bottom like some out-of-control submarine, plunged into the silt and rolled over, atop some of the trucks.

Two of the heavy-water containers, which had air locks, foamed to the disturbed surface. They were the only mute but telling evidence of the end to a German dream of world domination. . . .

Knut Haukelid read the severely censored reports on the front pages of the Oslo newspapers.

"Railway Ferry *Hydro* Sunk In The Tinnjö."

In London, "the Scoutmaster" marvelled, as he re-read the planning report from "Bonzo", how everything had worked out exactly as scheduled.

At Skien the "Chaffinch" group radioed a message of congratulations and British submarines lying in wait in the Skagerrak turned back for base.

In Rjukan hospital Kjell Neilsen, the Norsk Hydro engineer, came round from the anaesthetic to learn the news. He would have been the first suspect grabbed by the Gestapo in the reprisals so he arranged to have a perfectly healthy appendix removed, as the saboteurs drove to Mel.

Haukelid worried what the enemy would do to others once Himmler put on the pressure.

So far the heavy water had taken seventy-four lives. Thirty-four in "Operation Freshman". Twenty-two in the Flying Fortress raid. Eighteen in the doomed ferry.

CHAPTER 15

The Trolls Begin to Chuckle

HAUKELID reached the Swedish territory with Larsen, after a three-day struggle, by way of Norde Finnskogan. It was third time lucky over the wartime frontier for him, but for the engineer, who had left relatives behind, it was a first visit. Both men were deeply worried by the revenge the Gestapo would take for the sinking of the ferry.

Understandably, Haukelid savoured with rare appetite the luxuries of a return to civilised living. He got rid of his beard in double quick time, took advantage of the hot baths that were available day and night and sat back and enjoyed the fine meals that were served to him. It was good not to have to cook for one's self, or lumber around looking for fuel with frozen fingers. He liked the comfort of a soft bed in the hotel, which was a sounding box for all that was happening in Europe. Nor was there any lack of money—everything had been laid on in a handsome way.

One night over a few drinks he came to the conclusion that to become introspective was to invite punishment—it was wiser to leave everything to the trolls. Many of his best friends in the Linge Company had perished on the way back to freedom. The unit had lost almost a third of strength within a year—mowed down on landings along the coast, or sunk without trace between the Shetlands and the Norwegian skerries.

When he saw Gunnar Syverstad again, two days after reporting to "Auntie", the Bergen girl at the British Embassy, who mothered the Linge Company, he was shocked at the twitching face of a young man who had been so cool and calm on the ferry.

"We killed fourteen of our own," Gunnar said time and again, looking into the bottom of his emptied glass.

Haukelid guided him on a shopping and drinking spree. After the sub-zero temperatures, the clammy darkness and the starvation of the Hardanger Vidda, the centre of Stockholm was a flood-lit paradise of escapism. There was accumulated back-pay to spend and generous living expenses.

"Eat, drink and be merry for tomorrow we die," said Syverstad mournfully and morbidly at the end of the evening, when he had just been restrained from tossing an inquisitive local into the nearest canal.

They liked their new surroundings, but not some of the people.

"It was very difficult at times," admits Haukelid, a man who can generate a cold killing fury very quickly. "We were, in a sense, guests, and had to take pains not to abuse our hospitality. For some of us the humiliation of defeat in the field, then the surrender, still rankled, and an unthinking remark could touch off the explosion, like the munitions the Swedes were selling secretly to both sides."

His two weeks in Stockholm were almost a fortnight too long. After the first two or three days of indulgence he longed for his mountains again, where, he was sure, the trolls were doing sentry duty.

He went back with the legendary Max Manus, D.S.O., M.C. and Bar, code-named "the Angel" and the best limpet-mine man of all the Norwegians, to Oslo. They were weary and sated from well-deserved celebrating.

From the frontier to Oslo took eight days. They split up in the city but he met Rolf Sörlie on his way to Stockholm who told him that Einar Skinnarland was awaiting his return at Vinje. He had important news for his old friend.

Before Haukelid returned to his old stamping ground he met Colonel B. Øen[1], the senior Norwegian in Special Opera-

---

[1] Served with Special Operations Executive from 1942 to 1945. He was awarded the O.B.E. and many Norwegian decorations of great distinction.

tions Executive, who was paying a second visit to Stockholm that March. A few months before he had touched down to brief district chieftains (they could be likened to the Scottish Covenanters of earlier days) and potential leaders of what might be the shape of things to come and what was expected of them. Because of his contacts within Norway, and his penetrating appreciation of the changing scene there, Colonel Øen had become one of the men that the Gestapo wanted eliminated at any cost.

In the overcrowded Norwegian Legation, flooded by refugees, saboteurs, businessmen risking their lives in beating the Nazi blockade, Haukelid sometimes had his secret talks with the senior officer in the oddest of places owing to the fact that a room was not always available.

Colonel Øen warned him, and others, that the Germans might attempt to recruit Norwegian teenagers as a labour force and might even drill and dragoon them into machine-gun fodder for the Russian front. In addition to guiding the expanding Resistance in his district, Haukelid was advised to think along the lines of establishing hidden camps in the hills, if the lads had to run for it.

When Colonel Øen returned to London the information he returned with encouraged Colonel Wilson to feel that the war was swinging their way. Four possible alternative conditions under which Norway might be liberated had been fully considered and the duties and responsibilities resolved. Special mention had been made of the need to secure the organised protection of industrial plants and public utility services. Local arrangements to this end had been agreed, and Øen had promised adequate support from the United Kingdom. The question of supplying some form of temporary police service during the interval between German withdrawal or collapse and the arrival of the Allied forces had been agreed also. The Central Leadership had laid great stress on the need to institute certain local military actions against the occupying power and its tools, both to strengthen Resistance and direct a blow against the Gestapo. They held this view because of the increasing attacks on people in connection with labour mobilisation, and the intensified activity of the

Gestapo in different parts of the country. "They rightly argued this," said the courier as he handed Colonel Wilson a type-written slip of paper:

> *The Norwegian people wish to play a part in the fight against the enemy, and they will endure the sacrifices entailed by military actions on the part of the Home Organisation when these activities are based on rational instructions, when the situation at the time is taken into account, and when these actions are carried out under responsible leadership.*

The Oslo cell of the Linge Company cheekily arranged that Haukelid should be driven in style to Vinje, as the senior salesman for a rubber-goods factory.

The chauffeur was one of the executives of the firm, who had had exactly five minutes' instruction in handling a revolver before setting out.

There was a road block at Hokksund, the Oslo intelligence team had learned. It was the place where Haukelid had changed trains on the way to Stockholm. He now had radio components in his rucksack. They made a wide detour around the danger points, to arrive on time.

When he shared his city food with Skinnarland later at their re-union meal in the Nilsbu hut Haukelid learned that radio traffic from London had tapered off—but the trolls, on the other hand, must have been active.

Throughout every district within contact, underground Home Forces were growing, slowly but relentlessly, like the glaciers forging their way down to the fjords. They needed more leaders to help them, Haukelid decided.

Tor Bö had remained at his legal job in the food office, helping by remote control in the earlier stages of the year before. He was invited to join them in the mountains, and arrived with a bundle of stolen, vital ration cards.

Other patriots made more and more frequent appearances in the uplands as they sensed the rising wind of freedom.

"The headquarters hut was like a big railway station, with

tracks converging from all angles," says Haukelid. "Too well known in the area, and maybe becoming suspect by even the stupid Germans.

"We decided to build another hut on the Hamrefjell, where Haugland and Skinnarland had tented out. This was to become our secret base unknown to anybody. Skinnarland coaxed a farmer into building a considerable extension to his barn. Not all the timber hauled up from civilisation was for this purpose. Some of the material was dumped at agreed spots and we took it further into the hills."

The real menace in this operation was not roving enemy patrols—but ferocious Norwegian midges. "Two feet across the back," jokes Haukelid. "They could have carried off not one baby, but twins."

With loads of material paralysing their shoulders, both hands engaged, they were the perspiring prey of, it seemed, every insect in the south of Norway.

They slaved on, all hours of the day and moonlight, and succeeded in putting up their new hut in two weeks. It was not the biggest building in the world—ten feet by ten feet, sleeping three men in discomfort—but Colonel Wilson reckoned it was the most important dot on the map of Norway at that time.

Tor Bö had been a carpenter. Skinnarland, dam-builder across the world later, was a handyman. Haukelid could blast his way around most obstacles. Bamse, the elk-hound puppy, had grown into a big dog and was roundly cursed as a nuisance.

"We ought to slit his throat," growled Haukelid, when the playful hound had tripped him up for the tenth time. "He'll go looking for a bitch down in the valley and lead the Hun right back here." Then he smiled, as the dog nestled up to him.

They named the new hut of their creation—Skriubu. Around this time, Colonel Wilson had also established a new base. The Scandinavian set-up of Special Operations Executive had been forced, through expansion and through growing successes, to move to the less romantic surroundings of Oxford Square, London.

Their hazards were different, but shared, in a way, with their agents in the field. Midges—and the desperate bombing over London of the rapidly dwindling Luftwaffe. A friendly dog, who might lead the enemy patrol with machine-guns and hand-grenades, to surround the Skriubu hut, or the indiscreet disclosure over the "one for the five-barred gate" in Mayfair.

To his great satisfaction, Wilson was given a Norwegian War Room, complete with the latest maps, charts and graphs, in the new headquarters. This provided a day-to-day, at-a-glance appreciation of all situations in his overseas territories.

It was manned by regional specialists of the Norwegian Foreign Office Intelligence Department, by experts from the British Foreign Office, by Squadron-Leader C. Squires of the Royal Air Force, and others. Some of the unnamed shadowy figures, at times in widely varying uniforms, more often than not in black-market dark suits, supplied the details which filled in the picture. They were steered there regularly from different sources.

One Norwegian oil-tanker captain, a second generation American, navigated his way to Oxford Square, after a round-the-world trip, mainly in convoy, to tap in the vital statistics about current fuelling facilities likely at Bergen, Stavanger, Trondheim and elsewhere.

Wilson echoed the thinking of Churchill that all this was the beginning of the end. He had his problems and there were two formidable among them. One was the conference clashes with other foreign and American intelligence groups. The other was the need to give new agents in Norway a better chance of remaining alive. They were in danger from reprisals following misguided and often unrelated sabotage actions of a group known as the young "Activists".

Yet he was not unhappy that summer of 1944. He had begun to see the writing on the fresh-painted cream and green walls.

Their net was spreading and bringing in some strange, but useful big fish, from as far away as Australia. In one instance —a shark hunter around the corals of the Great Barrier Reef, who contributed some of the answers to underwater gliding, so that the limpet-mine instead of the knife did most damage in the shortest space of time.

The net-work itself was receiving more and more outside support from other groups in the Haukelid technique of ending the war quickly.

Some of Colonel Wilson's thinking, smothered perhaps by more senior memoirs afterwards, must be repeated. If just for the sake of belated Anglo-Norwegian post-war history.

Of the communications system which could have cost a life a mile within Norway, and many more sinkings between that country and Britain, he wrote: —

"The first essential for any form of clandestine operations is to establish reliable and quick channels. Within Norway, occasional use was made of the telephone system. This had dangers and could only be used sparingly and discreetly. In the more populated places the use of the telephone was valuable, particularly for sending warning messages.

"Since Milorg," he noted, "was in a position to listen in to German conversations, the Central Leadership was always conscious of the dangers of the telephone system and exercised the necessary control."

Every Resistance man was briefed time and again about the need for double-talk and of making the fullest use of code-names and a simple question-and-answer system. Briefly— "Hang up the receiver immediately if you hear a strange voice. Guttural or not."

"Sparing use was also made of advertisements and items of news in the papers," continued Wilson. "And this was difficult and subject to delay. Much more use was made of guards and drivers on the railway and places of concealment in railway coaches. Communications to Sweden freqently went by such means around this time.

"The normal system of internal communications was by courier. This was always subject to difficulties, dangers and delays. Both verbal and written messages were passed. The length of the last-named being governed by the amount of paper a man could swallow in a hurry!

"It was always difficult to appreciate in London how much time was required to pass a message from one part of the same district to another. In Gudbrandsdalen, for example, it might take a courier a week to travel along the top of the ridges and mountains and so avoid the patrols in the valleys. More often than not, insufficient time was allowed for a wireless station to have a message relayed by hand to a reception committee or operational party.

" Between Norway and the United Kingdom the channels of communication were many and various. The Special Operations Executive Mission in Stockholm was of great value in providing a quick method of communication by courier, then by telegraph or diplomatic bag to London. Members of the Linge Company also used Stockholm for a rest, or on leave, and their reports were written and transmitted from there. Many of them were flown back from Stockholm to Leuchars, but when aircraft priorities became more difficult and the time available for action more uncertain, proportionately fewer of the men were brought back to the United Kingdom. Possible operational necessity over-ruled personal preference.

" Communications between the west coast of Norway and the Shetlands gradually became speedier and more reliable. During the first two or three years the refugee traffic, although considerable, was not so productive of precise information as later. Couriers were sent across the North Sea and brought back again, but the information they obtained was limited. Later, the reverse was the case, and a number of most useful despatches were brought over by sea as the arrangements for rendezvous improved. Bergen was a case in point when very speedy and exact sea communications were established."

The men in the mountains were in high good humour for the first time since their country was forced to surrender. They ate well and slept well, healthily exhausted after covering long distances, to brief new recruits or survey yet another possible landing ground for the R.A.F. and the special squadron of the U.S.A.A.F. commanded by Colonel Balchen.

In Britain the build-up was accelerating, matching their mood. Supplies were the big headache. Colonel Wilson writes:

"The variety of operations and the different types of country and climate put a severe strain on the Supply Services. Standard containers and loads could be used for various re-supply operations, but no operational party could be sent to Norway from the United Kingdom with standard loads only. Each operation had to be separately mounted and equipped. Special equipment was obtained from ordinary Special Operations Executive sources, from Norwegian sources, from Sweden, and latterly from the United States. Skis, rucksacks, boots, mountain rations all had to be separately considered.

"Provision had to be made for the wide differences of temperature between summer and winter in Norway. The requests from the field for special stores were continuous and not half of them could be met. Every effort was made to give the field a reason when supplies could not be sent, but this was not always possible. Sometimes special supplies were dispatched but never arrived. The delay in the supply of Arctic equipment in the winter of 1944-1945 was serious and might have endangered many lives. Luckily the winter was not as severe or long as expected.

"Tobacco, coffee and chocolate were always in short supply. Many regard these as luxuries. To men living on mountain tops they were essentials. The biggest complaint of London's failure to supply sufficient tobacco came from a leader who was himself a non-smoker, but who realised the effect the lack of cigarettes and tobacco was having on the morale of his men."

Colonel Wilson singles out a trio from the Norwegian Section of the Special Operations Executive in Stockholm for special praise in keeping up the morale of his hunted and harried men.

"Mr. Neilsen, Mrs. Anne Waring and Mrs. Bernardes were all admirable in this respect and earned the thanks and affection of the men. These men had to be financed, clothed, equipped and speeded on their way. Stockholm carried out all the duties of a transit camp and reception centre, and it was all done in a friendly way which steadied nerves and revived tired bodies and minds."

Claus Helberg later endorsed this tribute.

"When I reached Stockholm with four of my proverbial nine lives squandered—the parachute drop, the ski chase, the crash over the cliff, the jump from the 'bus—after a rather pleasant but phoney piece of love-making, I was still pretty shaken. Then I just relaxed. Everything was so pleasant. I wanted to get back for further training but Stockholm was an oasis of relaxation for everybody."

Helberg, outwardly unchanged, Jens Poulsson and Arne Kjelstrup, were very important persons so far as the under-cover war effort was concerned.

They did not enjoy Stockholm for long. They had experience and vital knowledge, and several people lost their aircraft priority to take the saboteurs back for further training to Scotland and elsewhere.

Speaking of the men selected as agents in the field, Colonel Wilson says: "The changes of policy and of fortune through which the Norwegian Section of Special Operations Executive passed had a very considerable bearing on the men who were recruited into the Linge Company. At first, raids were favoured and the more fundamental work of helping to build up an internal underground organisation took second place.

"This entailed, when the raiding phase was over, the discharge of a number of men who were unsuitable for more patient and prolonged work. Common sense and adaptability are the two main virtues for anybody who has to work underground. At first a large number of misconceptions had to be overcome. The tough gangster of detective fiction was of little use. What was required was a man of character and high ideals, not necessarily expressed in terms of religion. It is curious how many members of the Linge Company imagined themselves to be atheists or agnostics, which was often far from being true.

"No normal course of training can determine a man's character. It is curious but true that some of the best members of the Linge Company were thought at first not likely to make good agents and one redoubtable member was almost rejected outright as unsuitable."

The Special Operations Executive basic and para-military training methods were continued through 1944 until men came back with added operational experience from the field. They were made instructors and the new intake was handed over to them to find the right material that later could be sent to help the Milorg groups.

Helberg, Poulsson and Kjelstrup found things had changed. They celebrated Haukelid's D.S.O. decoration in suitable fashion, then realised the poachers had turned gamekeepers.

Instead of sabotage, their next hazardous job was to be the saving of Norwegian installations at the moment of liberation and they were instructed in anti-demolition drill rather than the quickest way of blowing a building sky-high. They handled strange new weapons on the firing ranges and across the battle courses.

At the interviews with Colonel Wilson and Professor Tronstad they discovered the last-named elated by current achievements but worried about the final outcome. They were all to remember this.

Helberg, Poulsson and Kjelstrup had the feeling that they might see more of the soldier-scientist in their own country and fairly soon.

They went about their new tasks with mounting enthusiasm, parachute practice, propaganda instruction, guidance for local Resistance groups, taking apart and reassembling captured enemy weapons, memorising German phrases to meet any emergency and studying maps of Nazi dispositions throughout Scandinavia. And they all had new photographs taken, Helberg clowning as usual until the shutter was about to blink. Then he steadied up, stern-faced, in civilian clothing.

There is not all that difference between a camera aperture and the muzzles of a firing squad.

CHAPTER 16

The Longest Night

O<small>N</small> the Hardanger Vidda, Haukelid, Skinnarland and Tor Bö knew that their days of isolation were numbered and that events were now moving too fast for the enemy.

It was September, 1944, and they had read and read again a message from Colonel Wilson radioed from London. It said:

" Eight or ten, including several acquaintances, will arrive in the moon period at about the first. Two or three of them will make their headquarters with you, if you think this safe. Good luck."

Haukelid and Skinnarland, who was to continue as radio operator in the new set-up, thought back on the lonely beginnings when the fight back had only just begun.

Skinnarland remembered the desperate hi-jacking at sea of the *Galtesund*, the fresh air and fishy smell of freedom across the Aberdeen waterfront in March, 1942, the shove in the back over Ringway Airport, Manchester, and the dreary, drawn-out months between.

Haukelid never doubted then that his father's death through ill-treatment by the Nazis could have been prevented. Trond had struggled up from Oslo with the final news, as a tourist and bringing his wife with him to support the deception in case he was stopped and questioned.

So that glimpse, as he had ducked behind his friend's front door, when his father knocked, had been the last look. " The Gestapo," said Trond, " had discovered many miniature radio sets and components stowed by the Resistance, in the Haukelid store-room in the capital."

" Father knew nothing about these, but he did know about other underground activities," he told them in the hut. Proudly, he had declared, " HE wouldn't have told anyway. He would never have cracked."

He was right. He gave Trond a message with which to return to Oslo.

" Go back and tell the fellows that the time is coming."

Tor Bö, their latest leading recruit, looked from face to face. " I'll get some more wood for the store. Let's hope it is soon. I'm tired of fetching wood." He grinned as he went out.

In London, Major Leif Tronstad, having packed his kit, put away his few personal belongings in a small suit case to be stored in his absence. His documents were locked in Colonel Wilson's safe.

His main concern was the protection of all hydro-electric works in south-east Norway. The Norsk Hydro plant alone and the connecting water tunnels from the dam above, if expertly dynamited by the Germans, could sweep away half of Rjukan, four miles down the Maan gorge.

He had helped to master-mind the first destruction of the heavy-water stocks at the plant and now planned to safeguard, personally, this large wedge of Norway's post-war economic potential.

Major Tronstad had enlisted the services of Captain Norman P. Lind of the Royal Engineers, another poacher turned gamekeeper, to aid his fellow Norwegians. For many months, Lind had been training officers and men of the Linge Company in the niceties of sabotage and demolition. Now he was enthusiastic about his new job.

In Scotland, Poulsson, Kjelstrup and Helberg worked over their skis beneath the naked yellow bulbs, behind the blackout curtains, sand-papering, polishing and waxing, and it was about this time that Haukelid and Skinnarland, awaiting the new arrivals, were able, with great shouts of laughter, to study the photographs of their three old comrades, stuck to current identity cards, passed on from Oslo by way of a Rjukan courier.

" Poulsson is losing hair. Rapidly! "

" No wonder, it's the Scottish beer."

" Look at Kjelstrup. Public Enemy Number One."

The cards had correct names and numbers stolen from the Oslo controlled files—but the prints had been developed and processed in a Scottish police dark-room and bore not the remotest resemblance to the appearances of the Norwegians for whom ostensibly they were issued.

Colonel Wilson pays this tribute to the police and authorities in his undercover caravan:

" The Norwegian Section had many direct contacts with various civilian authorities in Scotland and Shetland. Some of these may be specially mentioned as having been of great assistance. The police in Inverness-shire, Aberdeen and Shetland, rendered splendid service and met every call willingly and cheerfully.

" The London, Midland and Scottish railway officials were most helpful, not only in regard to the traffic of men and stores, but also in allowing the use of railway lines and bridges for various schemes and courses in training. Mr. Malcolm Speir, the General Manager in Scotland, the traffic manager at Inverness, and the stationmaster at Aviemore, gave full support. The two civil airlines to Shetland had frequently to put up with sudden priorities and sudden cancellations. Their pilots often carried special packages for quick dispatch from Shetland to London.

" All these, and many other people, received letters of thanks from the Section after victory had been won, and it was most gratifying and encouraging to read the acknowledgements that were received and the praise contained in them for the Norwegian personnel the writers had come to know."

Colonel John Skinner Wilson, born 1888, son of the Very Rev. J. S. Wilson, Dean of Edinburgh, was the right man in the right job. He was educated at Watson College and at Glenalmond. His grandfather was one of the founders of this school. Forty-three of the family have carved their initials on the desks for posterity.

When he impressed security upon the Highland ghillie, who was guiding him around the potential Norwegian training areas earlier in the war, the old man looked him straight between the eyes.

"There'll be no careless cackle up here. You'll remember we kept Prince Charlie's secret for long enough. 'Sides we like Norwegians."

So did many others. The writer, in fact, was First Lieutenant to Lieutenant-Commander Oli Berhardt Egjar, D.S.C., R.N.R., of Tønsberg, Norway, a whaling man, who escaped to the Shetlands with others in a small boat.

During about eighteen months of convoy duty up and down the West African coast, with the Freetown Escort Force, they argued most days about dawn and dusk sights and are still the best of friends.

From the photographs on the pile of forged identity documents the Hardanger Vidda trio picked out Professor Tronstad and Gunnar Syverstad of Tinnsjö ferry fame. The other three they could not agree about, in the end decided that they did not know the faces for sure.

"That one is British."

Haukelid probably pointed at the passport-size print of Captain Lind of the Royal Engineers.

"Guests arriving—and no beds made," he mocked happily, looking at their three crumpled sleeping bags. "But we must prepare real Norwegian hospitality for our visitors."

Within a week of receiving the message from London he had stalked and slain two of the best beasts from cropping herds in the area. He removed the entrails and buried the carcases, still in their skins, in the natural deep freeze of a sheltered snow-bank. That nearly cost him three frost-killed fingers.

As a first course, he netted dozens of trout from the river, gutted them, and cached them. In the sub-zero temperatures of the rapidly-approaching winter, the nets needed keeping under the water most of the time, otherwise they became as resistant as wire mesh.

M

Quite suddenly the weather worsened and the men in the hut were reminded of the infuriating delay they themselves had experienced in Scotland. Instead of the R.A.F. Operations officer shrugging his shoulders and announcing to eager up-turned Norwegian faces, "Sorry, chaps. No operations to-night," Skinnarland had swivelled around from his set, after a brief transmission, and nodded confirmation to the other two. "You're right. No drops tonight."

At Leuchars, Wick, and other airfields, the rain rattled like machine-gun fire across the bulging bellies of the Nissen huts, and soaked the ground crews, who grumbled their way from the warmth and shelter. It dappled the screens of the bombers beyond the instrument panels, as pilots waited to drag back on the control columns.

Night after night the question and answer remained as frustrating as ever. It might be raining in Scotland, but the weather over the dropping zones was something worse than impossible. Low cloud, high winds, or rain slashed through with sleet. Sometimes, snow storms were predicted.

Haukelid had supervised the marking out of the new landing areas, given them code-names, and the information was radioed to London. Chiltern Court had replied with air-to-ground signals, but still the hand-picked reception committee had nothing to do but wait and try to remain calm.

In his *Skis Against The Atom* Haukelid says:

" We never had an opportunity of thanking in person those fellows who came over on moonlight nights. They gave us arms and equipment to take up the fight afresh, and they had from the very first given us something that we needed—a feeling of community with all the other soldiers in the war. Those great heavy bombers were the link between us and the free world."

Often the shivering men on the ground cleared twenty tons of snow for a dropping strip, only to hear the noise of the aircraft drain away into the surrounding hills. Once Haukelid and Skinnarland searched two weeks for the wreckage of a bomber which London reported had crashed in their area, killing the crew outright. They searched in vain. To this day the Hardanger Vidda has not yielded up the secret.

Haukelid himself almost lost his life on another expedition. He was alone when he twisted his knee, surveying a potential landing ground for the parachutists from overseas.

Crippled, he knew it was hopeless to put weight on his leg for the twenty-mile trip back to Skriubu. He crawled beneath a boulder and listened to his small radio for any signals about approaching aircraft. He was there five days, with only the scantiest of emergency rations.

No bomber came. He had his Krag rifle, but the reindeer kept out of range. He was worse than half-starved when he limped back to the base hut.

"Once again we were literally starving. All the store food had gone. We wondered if the bomber boys would ever deliver. It was difficult to judge which was the more important. The fellows—or the food.

"The new recruits were impatient. Were they never coming from across the North Sea? I was vexed too. It was a lousy autumn. Heavy rain, night after night. When the rain cleared, the clouds climbed down from the hills and tossed the unwelcome blanket over us. There was, of course, any amount of snow. In normal times that would have been natural and welcome, but it was all wrong for our joint purposes at the time.

"Then, after my knee had knitted up, we received the welcome signal from Chiltern Court. I was to go to Langsjöen to meet two men from Britain."

Haukelid suspected it might be his good friend Tor Vinje returning. It was. His companion was another Resistance fighter he knew, Erling Bestre. As the latter jerked on the cords to gentle his landing he roared happily from the air: — "I've brought the nappies[1]."

---

[1] Diaper delivery direct from Special Operations Executive headquarters. Along with plastic explosives, the latest in guerilla warfare weapons from all Allied sources. Rompers and rifles. Baby powder and powder of another sort. When the second baby was born to Mrs. Niels Krohg, who had been trained as a stand-in telegraphist by her husband, Colonel Wilson was heard to exclaim: —" If they make a habit of this they'll endanger security! " He repeated his little joke when he met the Krohg family in Oslo after it was all over. "Lovely children, And what better way for a good Norwegian to enter a troubled world."

"Don't wet yourself when you hit the deck," Haukelid shouted back.

It was a perfect landing, unlike so many on the treacherous terrain of Norway. Soft, yielding snow. Vinje and Bestre shed their parachutes and clasped hands seconds after their touchdowns. They brought food, coffee and tobacco in addition to arms, equipment and a complete layette for a new baby.

To Mrs. Krohg, the baby clothing was all important. To the menfolk, who had been rationing cigarette ends and the scrapings from pipe bowls, it was the tobacco which really counted!

Those on the ground had reindeer meat and preserved fish for the visitors, but the first meals together were made feasts with all the little civilised extras from the air.

And it was the beginning of the break-back. Events were marching in the mountains. Erling Bestre brought new guidance from Britain. They were to change from the defensive to a state of near readiness for the offensive.

Haukelid, so security-minded for so long, at first doubted the wisdom of establishing big bases in the uplands for the war training of men on the run, fugitives who, in the past, would have made their way to the safety of Sweden. Yet it was a heartening sign.

"The R.A.F. will pour in supplies when requested," said Erling, gnawing at his first reindeer bone for long enough. "I have to go west to Suldal and set up a base there. By now some of the other Linge boys should have landed on the Fyresdal moors with the same job to do. Others are coming."

Because there was little inter-communication across the vast and icy deeps of the Hardanger Vidda, except by leg-weary couriers, or by short-wave radio through the British monitoring stations, deliberately discouraged, Knut Haukelid was away organising his teams at the Skriubu base when "Sunshine" finally burst over their mountains.

The drop was achieved on the moonlit night of October 5th—6th, 1944. Nine dropped safely, bones intact, from two long-range aircraft.

"Once more out of the breach, dear friends," thought Claus Helberg, as he flowered out of the bomber's belly. Like the others, he never guessed how near he had been to disaster.

The drop had been delayed for a long month by the impossible weather conditions. Skinnarland, the most patient of men, had become exacerbated as, day by day, he talked to recruits with the fire of victory in their blood and he had pleaded with London for a special midnight message. His normal transmission had brought back the stock reply about no operations during the night. But the weather was improving by the minute at his end. He almost cursed into the key with his fingers.

"It was decided at the last moment to fly," Colonel Wilson reported, through the normal channels, to the War Cabinet. "This information was relayed to Skinnarland."

It was received, after delay, with mixed-up feelings. Skinnarland had scattered his reception group back to their farmhouses and hideouts.

Before he had time to finish one of his precious, hoarded cigarettes, he heard aircraft engines overhead.

"He dashed out on his skis," continued Wilson's report, "and set his reception flares. Single-handed, he received the whole party, who made a perfect landing."

As if to emphasise the hit-or-miss difficulties of all operations over Norway, the report added: "A third supply aircraft failed to find the spot."

Even so, twenty-four vital containers and six packages accompanied nine determined, experienced Norwegians back to their native snows, to help in finishing the war the way they wanted it ended. Quickly, and without too much loss of life or destruction of national property.

Major (Professor) Leif Tronstad was the leader, in his first parachute jump in action, although he had progressed from hangar falls, to captive balloons and low-circling training aircraft. Jens Poulsson was back again, as second-in-command, with Claus Helberg and Arne Kjelstrup.

Young Gunnar Syverstad had been attached, mainly as bodyguard to Tronstad, a man marked out by the Gestapo.

It was, without exaggeration, the greatest re-union ever to take place on the plateau, which can be so pleasant in the good months, such a death-trap in the bad. Tactical and other talk went into the late hours of the morning as they shared food and experiences.

Rumours had reached the Hardanger Vidda about a second miraculous escape by their old comrade, Knut Haugland, in Oslo, this time.

The men from overseas filled in the details, because Haugland had reported back to Chiltern Court. It appeared that the telegraphist for the earlier *Grouse* group had reached the underground of the capital from his Kongsberg man-hole.

"Colonel Wilson gave him the job of finding a ring of suitable sites for radio stations for the Central Leadership around Oslo," explained Tronstad. "And the canny old 'Scoutmaster' was able to help right from the beginning. One of his former Boy Scout associates supplied a list of pre-war Rover camping huts in the near-by hills and woods which were unmarked on any civilian map.

"Haugland began to train operators, local men, when overseas fellows were not available. He had to set up a special station to work himself, and for passing important messages from the Central Leadership to London direct."

"Slowly his luck began to run out, the way mine did," interjected Helberg.

Mid-way through December, Haugland moved into the flat of Doctor Finn Bøe at Rikshopital Kvinne Klinikken (The Maternity Hospital) and slept there. He had his set in the attic of the hospital, in a kind of niche. Dr. Bøe was not only a wonderful patriot, but a great cover man. He helped to code and de-code messages when there was a rush on from anywhere.

For three uneasy months Haugland played his luck to the full. On April Fool's Day in Britain he was forced into his longest transmission ever. Forty drawn-out minutes, tapping away with his right hand, glancing at the watch on his left wrist and rather desperately aware of the opportunity he was giving enemy radio direction-finding vans scouring the city below.

The information he passed was vital. His last code groups were to the effect that he planned to make the run for Stock-

holm shortly, to relay in greater detail the growing needs of the
Central Leadership. He signed off with relief. . . .

They were waiting for him. Five of them. One clicked on
the single electric bulb as he made his usual way through a
darkened passage. Many months in the wilds had quickened
his reactions, just that split-second which makes all the difference. He ducked and dropped back, in nearly the same
movement.

He scrambled back to his hide-out, up a flue and out of a
trap door in another wing. No bullets chased him but he could
hear sounds of pursuit, hoarse guttural instructions, feet trip-
ping over unexpected and unfamiliar obstacles.

There was only one stairway from the top floors of the
hospital to the attic. It was covered by two Germans.

He shot them both and took the stairs three at a time.

In the pause for breath at a corridor window he saw that
the front exits from the hospital were guarded. He ran down
a side stair, into a cellar, Another two of the enemy squad
barred his way. He hit at least one of them and burst out of
the back door.

Yet another two Gestapo men were a few feet away, with a
third closing in from the opposite direction.

The first couple turned and ran when he flourished his gun.
The other man ducked behind the corner of a building when
Haugland fired his last round at him. This gave the Resistance
man a chance to push in another loaded magazine.

From cover the third German emptied his revolver at a
range of about five yards and missed. Haugland ran for it,
jumped a wall, cleared the hospital grounds, ducked another
group of the converging enemy, skirted a naval sentry with a
rifle and disappeared into the streets of Oslo.

When he gave the special knock the door of a house opened,
and closed, quickly, behind him.

He was steered from one safe hiding place to the next, talking all the time with Milorg leaders about closer co-operation
with the United Kingdom, memorising their requests and
thinking.

Early in his strange, undercover pilgrimage he was gleefully
informed that he had killed three of the Gestapo and seriously

wounded two others in his escape. The senior, and hated,
Gestapo officer, who had failed to trap him in the hospital
siege, had been demoted on the scene. "Without any anesthe-
tic. Local or otherwise," they joked, and raised their glasses.

In the roundabout way, congratulations had arrived from
London and when Haugland's reply went back it contained
the usual understatement:

"Credit for my marksmanship must be given first and fore-
most to Major Sykes[1], who gave us excellent tuition. He always
laid stress on the fact that one shot, even from a heavy calibre
pistol, was not enough to put a man out of action completely.
My experience goes to show that one cannot feel safe until one
has made a good hit with at least two shots."

Haugland's desperate encounter was talked over for some
time, but as the hours wore on there were some awkward
pauses as when somebody began, "What happened to . . . ?"
Names began to trail away as they heard of friends who would
never be seen again.

Major Tronstad had the last word to say towards daylight
when, paternally it seemed, he remarked, "Numerically, we
have lost many men of the Linge Company. It seems so, because there are not many of us, and we have to remember
the work that has been done and what we are now trying
to achieve. Mathematically, the odds are against us. It could
hardly be otherwise."

He did not know then, glad to be back in Norway, that he
was foretelling his own end.

[1] Major Sykes was senior training officer to the Linge Company in Britain.
Haugland returned to London later and his work in improving communications in Norway did not go unrecognised. When he returned to his own
country after V-E Day he was " adopted " by the hospital from which he had
escaped and went back to stay with Professor and Mrs. Bøe. None of the
hospital wartime staff suffered by his activities. Professor Bøe was listening
in his sitting room to a B.B.C. broadcast when the shooting began.

CHAPTER 17

Death in the Cabin

I T happened so quickly and unexpectedly. The head of the man came round the door and then in a flash there was a hand with a gun. Jon Landsverk was unable to say how many shots he heard in quick succession because the noise bounced round the confined space of the cabin and the smell of cordite was strong enough to paralyse thought.

Gunnar Syverstad dropped to the floor, dying, and, in another room, Professor Leif Tronstad got up from a chair, There were more shots, but the explosions seemed less violent as Sheriff Lognvik of Rauland, held in the cabin as a collaborator, grabbed a carbine leaning against the wall and backed through the outer room to freedom.

It was all over in less than a minute and Landsverk saw that Syverstad, bleeding from the head, was hardly breathing. In the outer room he found Leif Tronstad dead. He, too, had been shot through the head. Although Landsverk was only a young recruit, inexperienced and overcome by the swiftness and finality of all he had witnessed, he knew what to do. He streaked away to find Skinnarland.

It was the wisest thing to do on that confused day of March 11th, 1945, because Tronstad's murder might well have triggered off a major but premature rising in one of the most vulnerable regions of Norway and even, perhaps, sparked off other powder kegs across the land—where powder was figuratively, still damp. But it was a desperately near thing.

Murder had been set in motion, quite literally, about a week before when Syverstad visited Sheriff Lognvik in his office. The young saboteur walked in quietly, took a seat opposite the sheriff, and put a pistol on the desk, just out of the reach of the pro-Nazi magistrate. He told him that ugly rumours were circulating in the district that could spell disaster for someone. With a wry smile, Syverstad looked at Lognvik and said it had been hinted, slanderously no doubt, that the *lensmann* had been probing in certain activities that did not really concern him in his official capacity. Picking up the gun and thumbing the chamber Syverstad said that according to rumour Lognvik was relaying the results to the Nazis.

"It's utter nonsense," protested the sheriff. The interview was quickly over. Lognvik promised to keep his eyes closed and his mouth shut and Syverstad left after picking up his pistol in a manner that indicated that the sheriff had made a wise decision.

The following day, contacts in Rauland passed along the information that Lognvik had telephoned German headquarters in Rjukan and that the conversation had lasted twenty minutes. Something had to be done about him—either executed or put where he could do no further damage.

The trap, which snapped back in such tragic fashion, was set that March morning. Landsverk went to Lognvik's office and reported a burglary at a certain hut, which he thought the sheriff should know about. He offered his services as a guide.

Once away from the houses Tronstad and Syverstad caught up with the two men and at gun-point they then took the collaborator to the Syrtebekk cabin near the Mösvatn.

Tronstad, a humane man, decided against outright killing. His prisoner would be lodged under guard in another hut in Kvendalen and kept there until the Resistance had dealt with the Nazis.

Then the shooting had begun. In the secret service files in London the deaths have been charged against "a half-witted relative" of Lognvik. Half-witted or not, his marksmanship was excellent.

When Landsverk found Skinnarland at the near-by Neset farm they returned without delay to the cabin to do what was urgent and necessary. Landsverk took up guard while the older man disposed of papers and anything that could be of value to the enemy.

When this was done, they found a sledge on which they laid the bodies of their comrades. They hauled the sledge to a tarn and through a hole in the ice the dead were laid to rest. Professor Leif Tronstad had been exactly 156 days back in the country he loved.

Skinnarland's mood was that of vengeance, but security, too, demanded that the collaborators should be headed off before they reached the enemy. Help was mobilised but the pursuit failed and Lognvik and his rescuer escaped the net.

So it was that the Nazi trucks, filled with grey figures sitting bolt upright, row by row, and who looked like toy soldiers through the binoculars of those who watched from secret places, roared into the uplands that the German troops dreaded and detested.

Haukelid did not hear news of the killings until the next day and the first report he received was completely garbled. It suggested that Lognvik had been shot and, as a result, Haukelid suspended all Milorg training in his area. A second message however revealed the truth. " Julius and Kaare," it said, "shot yesterday in encounter with magistrate Lognvik and another." These were the cover names for Tronstad and Syverstad.

There was further bad news, for Haukelid learned that the young men of Rauland had mobilised and this could mean big trouble.

" I was at my wits' end," confesses Haukelid. The premature head-on clash of arms he had dreaded seemed likely to happen. In the gathering dark he took two Sten guns from the nearest arms dump and went in search of Niels Krohg.

Krohg had heard about the enemy penetration, but not about the killings. As they talked Tor Bö arrived in a bus he had stolen. It was a solid hill-country Norwegian bus, which would be returned, undamaged, he hoped, to the rightful owners. Haukelid and Krohg got inside and the bus was driven towards the danger spot. They had to disperse the Resistance groups quickly or lead them to safety.

"Haukelid did a wonderful job when he came down from Vest-Telemark," says Claus Helberg, his old comrade in the raid on Norsk Hydro. "He prevented needless slaughter. Some of the Rauland fellows had only had a gun in their hands for five minutes. During that winter we had received wonderful support from the R.A.F. In drop after drop they had provided us with weapons and equipment for two thousand men. It was a splendid feat."

When Haukelid and the other two parked the bus by Grungedal, Niels Krohg was sent off to alert the local commander of Milorg. He also carried a message for transmission to London.

This read: "Deeply regret to inform you that Julius and Kaare have been killed according to a report from Rauland. German troops are in Rauland and the whole organisation and others have taken to the hills. Leaving tonight for the upper areas in Rauland to try to collect the Milorg men and take them to a safe place. Have taken all security measures in my district. Will give all the help I can."

In London, Colonel Wilson was shocked at the fate of the dedicated man he had worked with for so long.

The Anglo-Norwegian Collaboration Committee met swiftly to assess the damage to their efforts. They put on record: "Major Tronstad was a foundation member and showed at all times a lively sense of his duties. His constant good humour and his friendliness, combined with his enthusiasm and his special knowledge were of the greatest value to the Committee and to the work carried out under its aegis."

Colonel Wilson passed along a special minute to the War Cabinet about the murders.

"It was in this fashion that one of the best brains in Norway was denied to her post-war service. 'Sunshine' felt the loss more than any, but their considered opinion is that it was right that Leif Tronstad should have proceeded to Norway with them. It is necessary to record this. Major Tronstad was able to transmit information regarding German progress in atomic research and in other secret weapons, obtained from his scientific contacts."

Haukelid went over the mountains to Arabygdi with Tor Bö and a local scout and they arrived at first light to find armed men in every farmhouse and within a perimeter out on the ice. All were anxious to come to grips with the enemy. It was a situation that could hardly have been more disquieting. Too early was as bad as too late and the latest intelligence was that probing enemy patrols were only two miles away.

Einar Skinnarland had moved eastwards to tell Jens Poulsson that he was the new leader of the "Sunshine" group. Haukelid sent for Björn Gardsjord, the local platoon commander and called together the various section leaders. He said to them bluntly:

"For almost two years some of us have been working under cover so that our friends and relatives would not suffer another Televaag tragedy. It is not yet the right time. We must take to the hills before there is a clash that is certain to go against us. There is food enough up there. Don't expect any comfort. You'll be overcrowded, but better a little discomfort than to bring disaster on those who have helped us."

He divided what money he had among the four older men and told them to buy all the food the near-by farmers could spare.

They assembled in sections and then moved off in Indian file, a big gap between each man. Some of them went to the area around the Songevatn, having been warned to duck any fighting. Haukelid and Tor Vinje led thirty of them on a two-day march over to the south side of the Haukeli road. Most of the men dropped in their tracks when they reached the chosen huts.

Their leader's first anxiety, even before food, was to reestablish contact with Poulsson and Skinnarland, to let them know how the Rauland men had been spirited away and dispersed, and how quickly and in what numbers they could be called upon in any emergency.

This was done through London by radio.

" I was telegraphist with Poulsson at the time," recalls Helberg. " We were down in the Rjukan area, but not too close, nor were we seen too often in the streets by the folk who had known us from childhood.

" The main task of 'Sunshine' was to protect the factories and power-stations in the Rjukan-Notodden-Nore triangle, where at least sixty per cent of the electro-chemical industry of Norway was based.

" The Professor's death seemed to give a strange impetus to our activities. Skinnarland came to join us, with Captain Lind, who chatted away like a Norwegian.

" At this period, after the killings, some of the boys branched out a bit. To my knowledge there was sabotage which might not otherwise have happened, or quite so soon. Railway stock and power stations were blown up and tracks immobilised. A Fiesler Storch scouting plane at the small Acrå airfield was knocked out, to discourage inquisitive pilots. But possibly the most telling damage was among the anti-aircraft crews. Twenty-seven 88-mm shells in all were 'treated', without the Germans discovering they were distributing ammunition, loaded with highly-dangerous plastic explosive, to their own men."

At this time these were the dispositions of the " Sunshine " sub-groups.

" Moonlight "—Poulsson, Helberg, Skinnarland and Lind in the Rjukan area. In the Nore district with headquarters at Numedal, Arne Kjelstrup and newcomer Eldar Hagen (code-name " Starlight "). In the Notodden area " Lamplight " —Herluf Nygard and Leif Brönn.

" I received a signal from London arranging a meeting between Poulsson, Skinnarland and Haukelid," continues Helberg. " They discussed in detail what would happen in the event of fighting or German capitulation. Events were as far advanced as that.

" Skinnarland was worried, rightly concerned, about the fate of the Mösvass dam he knew so well This stood out as the main demolition target behind retreating Germans. The Rauland boys were assigned the task of wiping out any enemy dynamiting parties when the moment came.

" This was by no means as easy as it sounds," says Haukelid. " Obviously the Nazis would send in tough covering forces. Our men were keen and eager, their tails were up, but they were less than half-trained to tackle professional soldiers."

From this situation stemmed one of the most audacious plans of the war within Norway. The enemy had cordoned off the Hardanger Vidda, content with placing guards at all likely road and track blocks, and working to the principle that if the capture and destruction of the mountain men was impossible, they at least could be contained.

What better place then for a training sanctuary than within the German-defined area?

At the beginning of April, 1945, about two hundred volunteers, from Rauland and elsewhere, were transferred eastwards to Songevatn. Not for nothing had Knut been nicknamed " the General " at Aviemore, Scotland.

The new camp was run on strictly military lines, with training schedules, orders-of-the-day in writing and a quartermaster's store. Perhaps the biggest difference with the training Norwegians had received in Britain was that live ammunition was now used in all exercises.

Local commanders reported for a course of instruction and then returned to their own village cells. Food was a problem. Only meat was unrationed. In one period of twelve days, reported the quartermaster proudly, the men had devoured thirty-two reindeers.

Haukelid, when he was not lecturing about the swiftest and most silent ways of killing Germans, led big hunting parties. The bread-and-butter diet was solved by ingenuity and the whole-hearted co-operation of the small communities which surrounded them, but who lived beyond the enemy lines. Haukelid hinted at requisition orders likely to arrive from London and persuaded the food officer at Vinje to place 4,500 lb of flour at the camp's disposal—for withdrawal as needed. This was frequent for they ate fifty home-baked loaves a day.

Hoarded butter, made during the winter months, and knitted woollers, reached them from the womenfolk, who realised that, at last, something would stir with the coming of spring in the uplands.

In the same spirit shopkeepers sent up tobacco and what coffee they could spare. None of them knew where these luxuries, passed along by messengers, would finish up. But they had a good idea they would go to billets where they were most needed.

CHAPTER 18

Liberation—and Postscript

O N the eighth and ninth days of May, 1945, the bulk of the Norwegian Home forces and the Resistance leaders in hiding, having heard Churchill's momentous announcement of victory in Europe, came out into the open to set about the task to which they had dedicated themselves—none more so than the men who had been parachuted into the country and, throughout the years, had undergone unbelievable privations and perils in the fight for freedom.

The anti-Nazi forces needed no rallying in the retaking of their country and the 50,000 who mustered for the job were mostly young men—very young men.

At once they began to seize control of all strategic points, demanded the surrender of German garrisons and stepped in to prevent demolition and wanton destruction. They had some powerful arguments in their hands, for in the four months from the beginning of the year, in fact on all nights when flying was possible, they had received 2,250 Bren guns, 3,500 Sten guns, 17,500 rifles, 2,000 carbines, 50,000 lb of explosives and more than five million rounds of ammunition.

Thirteen aircraft had failed to return from these operations.

In anticipation of the week of the rising, British Intelligence sources had supplied a detailed list of enemy strength and dispositions in Norway.

The 20th Army, allied to the remainder of the 21st Army Group—most of which had been siphoned off for the fighting in France—was around 100,000 officers and men. German naval strength was not easy to calculate. Bergen, Trondheim and Narvik, in that order of importance, remained the permanent operational bases. Horten, Kristiansand and Stavanger were transit, testing and repair centres. Fresh consignments of one-man torpedoes and explosive boats had been distributed along the west coast, and most of them were at Stavanger and Molde.

Anti-aircraft defences in south Norway, particularly in Oslofjord, had been strengthened.

The break-down of the estimated number of German and quasi-German Armed Forces and civilians in Norway was as follows:

> Army—200,000.
> Navy—85,000.
> Air Force—50,000.
> S.S. and Police—5,000.
> Para-military—12,000.
> Civilians—10,000.

The number of prisoners-of-war behind barbed wire and machine-gun turrets scattered across the country had been a further problem for the Milorg leaders. They knew that men who had become desperate through torture and hunger, once they secured freedom, might break out to loot and rape the country.

From information secured by both the Norwegians and the British, the Resistance leaders knew of the presence of no less than 85,000 Russians, 2,000 Yugoslavs and about the same number of Polish prisoners. These nationalities were an unpredictable factor, but no fears were entertained about the release of British prisoners-of-war, who could be relied upon to come to the support of the liberators, as would the majority of 4,000 Dutch in the south and pockets of Danes, French and Belgians.

The Central Leadership had also been advised that massed help could be expected from Britain under the command of General Sir Andrew Thorne, Commander-in-Chief, Scotland, who had been nominated by S.H.A.E.F. Additionally, police troops, trained secretly in Sweden, were ready to move over the border at the drop of a fur hat.

To guard against the possibility of betrayal within the country the "Sunshine" group had evolved a plan, drafted by Skinnarland and Captain Norman Lind of the Royal Engineers, and endorsed by Special Operations Executive. It was aimed at protecting life and property—especially the major industrial plants in Upper Telemark and the Kongsberg area. It called for (1) Counter-espionage by using loyal personnel in the plants; (2) Halting German demolition squads by armed opposition inside the plants and by destroying or neutralising German troops in the area; (3) Defence against German counter-attacks.

As events turned out there were no counter-attacks in their district, and Skinnarland and Captain Lind were later able to record: "It should be borne in mind that our forces were superior to those of the enemy in the area, numerically and in armament. The quality of the enemy troops was poor and there were no S.S. troops."

It was different elsewhere, particularly in the tensed-up Bergen region, but this Norwegian-Anglo planning-on-the-spot set the pattern of liberation for the whole country.

"Counter Sabotage. Our greatest help in this was the German *Wehrwirtschaft* plans. These demanded that anti-sabotage guards should be placed on all important industrial plants. Thus we were able to have our men inside all major targets at all hours of the day and night. They had weapons concealed inside. The Germans had ordered that all windows and entrances but one be bricked up. As a result, our guards inside the plants had every opportunity to prevent demolition. Emergency cut-outs, which would stop machinery as quickly as possible, were installed wherever possible and main switches for the lighting system were put in suitable places so that the enemy demolition squads, unfamiliar with the plant, would have to work in the dark.

"Dummy demolitions were planned wherever possible, particularly at Rjukan and Vemork power stations, where prepared charges were stored away for blowing down the roofs. In the case of Saaheim power station at Rjukan, these charges could have been placed weeks beforehand as the roof trusses are concealed from below by a false ceiling.

"The most important buildings were fitted with a piped or bottled supply of ammonia gas which could be used to flood the building and make it uninhabitable."

They took no chances and thought of almost everything. These tactics were duplicated all over Norway.

"Complete sets of plans and drawings of the target plants were hidden away. Where possible, vital spare parts were moved away for safety, and new telephone lines installed to speed up the warning system in the event of German action.

"Because of our local knowledge and awareness of German dispositions, we considered that our troops could in every case reach undetected a position for attack at close range. By simultaneous attack from several quarters, and by using superior fire power, we considered that the enemy would soon give up the struggle. The troops we had to contend with were mainly anti-aircraft units and Norwegian S.S. of rather low morale.

"The time required for mobilisation and getting into action," continue Skinnarland and Lind, "varied between eight and thirty-six hours, according to the targets. We had to reckon with the possibility that the mobilisation order would go by courier and the troops assemble and move up on foot.

"So that co-ordination in the district could be as good as possible, our lines of communication were, whenever practicable, covered by courier, telephone and radio. Operational orders for each target and each unit were written beforehand and ready for use on the addition only of a zero hour and date."

Apart from a few haphazard shots by trigger-happy German guards, which did no damage, the plan for their district worked out splendidly. Further afield, but in the closest touch through the warning net-work, Knut Haukelid had enjoyed one of his three big moments of the five-year war.

First of all there had been that instant when the soft explosion of the heavy-water plant sounded above the subdued whine of machinery at Vemork. Then came the headlines about the sinking of the ferry. He had read and read again that censored report, with mixed feelings. Decent Norwegians had died, to defeat a Nazi dream of far-flung conquest. Finally he had picked up the telephone, called the supposed secret number of the near-by German garrison, and instructed the Commandant there exactly when and how he should surrender his men and equipment!

There had been no argument at the other end of the line. Like so many Germans in Norway, who had lived comfortably and without thought of the day when the bill would have to be paid, he was astonished to find that things had come to an end. At first the Commandant could not believe he was being deposed by a disciplined force.

"It was wonderful to walk down the main street of my own town, Rjukan, again," says Claus Helberg, "in broad daylight and without fearing that grip on the shoulder. Old folks I might have forgotten came up and clasped me by the hand."

Because of the delay in settling details of the German surrender overseas, it took several days to achieve Norwegian liberation. The Legation in Stockholm relayed the order from London for the police troops there to move across the border and converge on Narvik, Trondheim and Oslo.

Lieutenant-Colonel C. S. Hampton of Special Forces, flew with Brigadier Hilton, in charge of disarmament, in a Sunderland aircraft and arrived in Oslo on the night of May 8th. At the Bristol Hotel in the city they met the Milorg leaders, with the German General Staff for Norway hovering in the background.

Special Forces sub-detachments reached Oslo and Stavanger by air two nights later. The groups for Kristiansand and Bergen reached Stavanger at the same time and motored to their destinations. In Bergen the situation was tense at first. General Thorne, contacted by Special Operations Executive, gave permission for Resistance men elsewhere to take over the seaport and they got there after a forced march.

At another west coast town it was realised that there was no prospect of Allied forces arriving for at least ten days, perhaps longer. Thousands of Germans were in the district and the situation was highly explosive until a quick-witted officer of the Linge Company, who earlier had been issued with a Sub-Lieutenant's (R.N.V.R.) uniform in the Shetlands as part of his masquerade, marched up to the local Commander and formally demanded surrender. With considerable heel-clicking this was achieved and the enemy troops were disarmed.

At Bodg, a hundred Milorg men faced no less than forty thousand of the enemy, and the additional worry of unknown numbers of prisoners-of-war in their area. They, too, had only a passing acquaintance with the carbines, pistols and hand-grenades they hefted and tested—weapons smuggled over the Swedish border ten days before V-N Day.

They put on a bold enough front, however, and the District Leader, with the co-operation of a loyal Norwegian Chief of Police, demanded the attendance of the German Commander.

He arrived stiffly, with five of his staff. Two of them had machine-guns at the ready as they entered the room. The house was ringed by fifty enemy troops.

The performance was so theatrical that the Norwegians smiled broadly. Although unarmed, preparations had been made to deal with any intransigence. The leader laid down the conditions of surrender; they were accepted, and guns and rifles were stacked.

Colonel J. S. Wilson's proudest hour was when he marched, with the Linge Company, past the late King Haakon in Oslo on June 7th, 1945, exactly five years to the day when the King had left to continue the war from Britain.

In his diary Wilson writes: "Fifteen thousand members of Milorg from all parts of south Norway marched past the King in front of the Palace. With the King were the Crown Prince and his family, General Ruge, General Øen and Jens Christian Hauge (Resistance leader) in battle-dress for the first time. The parade was a most inspiring sight. The uniforms and the weapons carried were varied in the extreme. The number and variety of the weapons astonished the crowd of spectators. An interesting feature was the wide-spread use of code-names as shoulder flashes and on helmets. 'Bjørn West' and 'Polar Bear' and 'Lark' caught the eye. The members of the Linge Company marched with the men they had helped to train."

Colonel Wilson, with Commander Unger Vetlesen,

U.S.N.R., Norwegian-born American, detached from the Overseas Strategic Service, was presented to the King and thanked for the assistance which had led to his return to Norway.

Before they stood down the Linge Company had expressed a wish to parade for the time as a unit before their monarch.

Colonel Wilson's diary continues: —

"The Norwegian Army took up the request and transformed it into a march past before the King of all irregular units sent into Norway during the German occupation from the United Kingdom and from Sweden. This brought in various members of the Naval and Military Intelligence services.

"On the morning of June 28th, 205 officers and other ranks of the Linge Company headed the march past, followed by sixty officers and ratings from the three submarine-chasers ordered round from the west coast for the purpose. (Based for most of the war in the Shetlands) The Special Naval Unit caught the public's imagination and they were given a special and well-deserved ovation.

"The Norwegian Army Command gave lunch to all who were on parade and to special Allied officers who had been engaged with them. The King was present and the Crown Prince thanked everyone for their services, referring to the work on which each unit had been engaged. He dwelt at length on the services of the Linge Company, and paid a tribute to Captain Martin Linge, whose son was present. He, too, had become a member of his father's Company and been sent into Norway. He was captured in January, 1945, and liberated in Germany. The Crown Prince also paid tribute to the Shetland crews and thanked the British and U.S. officers for their practical assistance to Resistance in Norway and emphasised that the Home Forces owed their existence to the work done from the United Kingdom."

They drank the last toasts, and pushed aside the napkins. Colonel Wilson inspected the Linge Company in billets at their request for the final time.

With General Thorne, he carried out visits to the Home Forces in south Norway and along the west coast from

Stavanger to Bergen, and Aalesund to Trondheim. Wilson met many who had only been code-names in the past.

Within a week of his return to Chiltern Court news of what had happened to Hiroshima sent him to his safe. He brought out a file of " Most Secret " documents. On top was a paper written August 10th, 1943, which prophesied: " From the information available it appears that it will take two years before the results of this product are brought into actual military operation."

Professor Tronstad had not lived to see his words come true. Wilson thought back. Snow blizzards and blossoming parachutes. The Allies had been right on the target date suggested by his old colleague. The enemy could have been many, many months ahead.

" But for these men . . ." The words, spoken aloud, trailed away. He locked the papers back in the safe. His war in London was almost over.

In the mountains he loved Haukelid was showing Major General William Hansteen, K.B.E., Supreme Commander-in-Chief of the Norwegian Armed Forces, some of his favourite fishing pools. A staff officer arrived with documents for signature. He brought the news.

After a few minutes conversation Hansteen turned to Haukelid.

" Have you ever heard of a Japanese city called Hiroshima? " A shake of the head.

"You will," said the General grimly. " It has been wiped off the map by an atomic bomb."

" They have really done it, it is the end of the war."

Haukelid slowly filled his pipe and thought that Norwegians had not died in vain.

The other officer might have guessed what he was thinking.

" Yes," he said slowly, " had it not been for you fellows that bomb might have exploded over the heart of London a long time ago. Might even have been left in a suit-case in Grand Central Station, New York. to blow the whole of Manhattan to hell . . ."

INDEX